✓ P9-CFE-767

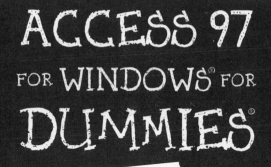

# ACCESS 97
## FOR WINDOWS® FOR
# DUMMIES®

*Quick Reference*

## by Alison Barrows

IDG Books Worldwide, Inc.
An International Data Group Company

Foster City, CA ✦ Chicago, IL ✦ Indianapolis, IN ✦ New York, NY

# Access 97 For Windows® For Dummies® Quick Reference

Published by
**IDG Books Worldwide, Inc.**
An International Data Group Company
919 E. Hillsdale Blvd.
Suite 400
Foster City, CA 94404
www.idgbooks.com (IDG Books Worldwide Web site)
www.dummies.com (Dummies Press Web site)

Library of Congress Catalog Card No.: 96-79263

ISBN: 0-7645-0056-2

Printed in the United States of America

10 9 8 7 6 5 4 3

1P/RQ/RR/ZY/IN

Distributed in the United States by IDG Books Worldwide, Inc.

Distributed by Macmillan Canada for Canada; by Transworld Publishers Limited in the United Kingdom; by IDG Norge Books for Norway; by IDG Sweden Books for Sweden; by Woodslane Pty. Ltd. for Australia; by Woodslane (NZ) Ltd. for New Zealand; by Addison Wesley Longman Singapore Pte Ltd. for Singapore, Malaysia, Thailand, Indonesia and Korea; by Norma Comunicaciones S.A. for Colombia; by Intersoft for South Africa; by International Thomson Publishing for Germany, Austria and Switzerland; by Toppan Company Ltd. for Japan; by Distribuidora Cuspide for Argentina; by Livraria Cultura for Brazil; by Ediciencia S.A. for Ecuador; by Ediciones ZETA S.C.R. Ltda. for Peru; by WS Computer Publishing Corporation, Inc., for the Philippines; by Unalis Corporation for Taiwan; by Contemporanea de Ediciones for Venezuela; by Computer Book & Magazine Store for Puerto Rico; by Express Computer Distributors for the Caribbean and West Indies. Authorized Sales Agent: Anthony Rudkin Associates for the Middle East and North Africa.

For general information on IDG Books Worldwide's books in the U.S., please call our Consumer Customer Service department at 800-762-2974. For reseller information, including discounts and premium sales, please call our Reseller Customer Service department at 800-434-3422.

For information on where to purchase IDG Books Worldwide's books outside the U.S., please contact our International Sales department at 650-655-3200 or fax 650-655-3297.

For information on foreign language translations, please contact our Foreign & Subsidiary Rights department at 650-655-3021 or fax 650-655-3281.

For sales inquiries and special prices for bulk quantities, please contact our Sales department at 650-655-3200 or write to the address above.

For information on using IDG Books Worldwide's books in the classroom or for ordering examination copies, please contact our Educational Sales department at 800-434-2086 or fax 317-596-5499.

For press review copies, author interviews, or other publicity information, please contact our Public Relations department at 650-655-3000 or fax 650-655-3299.

For authorization to photocopy items for corporate, personal, or educational use, please contact Copyright Clearance Center, 222 Rosewood Drive, Danvers, MA 01923, or fax 978-750-4470.

is a trademark under exclusive license to IDG Books Worldwide, Inc., from International Data Group, Inc.

# About the Author

**Alison Barrows** has taken the long route to ...*For Dummies* writing, most recently thinking she would have a career in economics. But over the years, an irresistible magnetic force, personified by friends who are ...*For Dummies* authors, has pulled her into the world of computers and technical writing.

Alison has been a serious computer user since high school (although she was too young to play with vacuum tubes, when they were the thing) and continued to use them at college. In college, thanks to some of the aforementioned friends, she worked at a software company, and after graduation went to the World Bank as a software guru. Her first foray into technical writing was at the World Bank, where she wrote training material for a two-day course which she then taught once a month. More recently, she has co-authored *Dummies 101: WordPerfect 6.1 For Windows* and *Dummies 101: WordPerfect 7 For Windows 95* and authored *Dummies 101: Lotus 1-2-3 97 For Windows 95*.

Alison has a master's degree in Public Policy from the Kennedy School at Harvard University and a B.A. from Wellesley College. In real life, she loves to sing, watch *Star Trek* (the newer versions), cook, and dabble in yoga, rock climbing, and Ultimate Frisbee. She currently lives in Gardner, Massachusetts, with her fiancé, Matt, and juggles writing computer books with planning a fast-approaching wedding.

# ABOUT IDG BOOKS WORLDWIDE

Welcome to the world of IDG Books Worldwide.

IDG Books Worldwide, Inc., is a subsidiary of International Data Group, the world's largest publisher of computer-related information and the leading global provider of information services on information technology. IDG was founded more than 25 years ago and now employs more than 8,500 people worldwide. IDG publishes over 275 computer publications in over 75 countries (see listing below). More than 90 million people read one or more IDG publications each month.

Launched in 1990, IDG Books Worldwide is today the #1 publisher of best-selling computer books in the United States. We are proud to have received eight awards from the Computer Press Association in recognition of editorial excellence and three from *Computer Currents'* First Annual Readers' Choice Awards. Our best-selling *...For Dummies*® series has more than 50 million copies in print with translations in 38 languages. IDG Books Worldwide, through a joint venture with IDG's Hi-Tech Beijing, became the first U.S. publisher to publish a computer book in the People's Republic of China. In record time, IDG Books Worldwide has become the first choice for millions of readers around the world who want to learn how to better manage their businesses.

Our mission is simple: Every one of our books is designed to bring extra value and skill-building instructions to the reader. Our books are written by experts who understand and care about our readers. The knowledge base of our editorial staff comes from years of experience in publishing, education, and journalism — experience we use to produce books for the '90s. In short, we care about books, so we attract the best people. We devote special attention to details such as audience, interior design, use of icons, and illustrations. And because we use an efficient process of authoring, editing, and desktop publishing our books electronically, we can spend more time ensuring superior content and spend less time on the technicalities of making books.

You can count on our commitment to deliver high-quality books at competitive prices on topics you want to read about. At IDG Books Worldwide, we continue in the IDG tradition of delivering quality for more than 25 years. You'll find no better book on a subject than one from IDG Books Worldwide.

**IDG BOOKS WORLDWIDE**

John Kilcullen
CEO
IDG Books Worldwide, Inc.

Steven Berkowitz
President and Publisher
IDG Books Worldwide, Inc.

*Eighth Annual
Computer Press
Awards ≥1992*

*Ninth Annual
Computer Press
Awards ≥1993*

*Tenth Annual
Computer Press
Awards ≥1994*

*Eleventh Annual
Computer Press
Awards ≥1995*

IDG Books Worldwide, Inc., is a subsidiary of International Data Group, the world's largest publisher of computer-related information and the leading global provider of information services on information technology. International Data Group publishes over 275 computer publications in over 75 countries. More than 90 million people read one or more International Data Group publications each month. International Data Group's publications include: **ARGENTINA:** Buyer's Guide, Computerworld Argentina, PC World Argentina; **AUSTRALIA:** Australian Macworld, Australian PC World, Australian Reseller News, Computerworld, IT Casebook, Network World, Publish, Webmaster; **AUSTRIA:** Computerwelt Osterreich, Networks Austria, PC Tip Austria; **BANGLADESH:** PC World Bangladesh; **BELARUS:** PC World Belarus; **BELGIUM:** Data News; **BRAZIL:** Annuário de Informática, Computerworld, Connections, Macworld, PC Player, PC World, Publish, Reseller News, Supergamepower; **BULGARIA:** Computerworld Bulgaria, Network World Bulgaria, PC & MacWorld Bulgaria; **CANADA:** CIO Canada, Client/Server World, ComputerWorld Canada, InfoWorld Canada, NetworkWorld Canada, WebWorld; **CHILE:** Computerworld Chile, PC World Chile; **COLOMBIA:** Computerworld Colombia, PC World Colombia; **COSTA RICA:** PC World Centro America; **THE CZECH AND SLOVAK REPUBLICS:** Computerworld Czechoslovakia, Macworld Czech Republic, PC World Czechoslovakia; **DENMARK:** Communications World Danmark, Computerworld Danmark, Macworld Danmark, PC World Danmark, Techworld Denmark; **DOMINICAN REPUBLIC:** PC World Republica Dominicana; **ECUADOR:** PC World Ecuador; **EGYPT:** Computerworld Middle East, PC World Middle East; **EL SALVADOR:** PC World Centro America; **FINLAND:** MikroPC, Tietoverkko, Tietoviikko; **FRANCE:** Distributique, Hebdo, Info PC, Le Monde Informatique, Macworld, Reseaux & Telecoms, WebMaster France; **GERMANY:** Computer Partner, Computerwoche, Computerwoche Extra, Computerwoche FOCUS, Global Online, Macwelt, PC Welt; **GREECE:** Amiga Computing, GamePro Greece, Multimedia World; **GUATEMALA:** PC World Centro America; **HONDURAS:** PC World Centro America; **HONG KONG:** Computerworld Hong Kong, PC World Hong Kong, Publish in Asia; **HUNGARY:** ABCD CD-ROM, Computerworld Szamitastechnika, Internetto online Magazine, PC World Hungary, PC-X Magazin Hungary; **ICELAND:** Tolvuheimur PC World Island; **INDIA:** Information Communications World, Information Systems Computerworld, PC World India, Publish in Asia; **INDONESIA:** InfoKomputer PC World, Komputek Computerworld, Publish in Asia; **IRELAND:** ComputerScope, PC Live!; **ISRAEL:** Macworld Israel, People & Computers/Computerworld; **ITALY:** Computerworld Italia, Macworld Italia, Networking Italia, PC World Italia; **JAPAN:** DTP World, Macworld Japan, Nikkei Personal Computing, OS/2 World Japan, SunWorld Japan, Windows NT World, Windows World Japan; **KENYA:** PC World East African; **KOREA:** Hi-Tech Information, Macworld Korea, PC World Korea; **MACEDONIA:** PC World Macedonia; **MALAYSIA:** Computerworld Malaysia, PC World Malaysia, Publish in Asia; **MALTA:** PC World Malta; **MEXICO:** Computerworld Mexico, PC World Mexico; **MYANMAR:** PC World Myanmar; **NETHERLANDS:** Computer! Totaal, LAN Internetworking Magazine, LAN World Buyers Guide, Macworld Netherlands, Net, WebWereld; **NEW ZEALAND:** Absolute Beginners Guide and Plain & Simple Series, Computer Buyer, Computer Industry Directory, Computerworld New Zealand, MTB, Network World, PC World New Zealand; **NICARAGUA:** PC World Centro America; **NORWAY:** Computerworld Norge, CW Rapport, Datamagasinet, Financial Rapport, Kursguide Norge, Macworld Norge, Multimediaworld Norge, PC World Ekspress Norge, PC World Nettverk, PC World Norge, PC World ProduktGuide Norge; **PAKISTAN:** Computerworld Pakistan; **PANAMA:** PC World Panama; **PEOPLE'S REPUBLIC OF CHINA:** China Computer Users, China Computerworld, China InfoWorld, China Telecom World Weekly, Computer & Communication, Electronic Design China, Electronics Today, Electronics Weekly, Game Software, PC World China, Popular Computer Week, Software Weekly, Software World, Telecom World; **PERU:** Computerworld Peru, PC World Profesional Peru, PC World SoHo Peru; **PHILIPPINES:** Click!, Computerworld Philippines, PC World Philippines, Publish in Asia; **POLAND:** Computerworld Poland, Computerworld Special Report Poland, Cyber, Macworld Poland, Networld Poland, PC World Komputer; **PORTUGAL:** Cerebro*PC World, Computerworld/Correio Informático, Dealer World Portugal, Mac*In*PC*In Portugal, Multimedia World; **PUERTO RICO:** PC World Puerto Rico; **ROMANIA:** Computerworld Romania, PC World Romania, Telecom Romania; **RUSSIA:** Computerworld Russia, Mir PK, Publish, Seti; **SINGAPORE:** Computerworld Singapore, PC World Singapore, Publish in Asia; **SLOVENIA:** Monitor; **SOUTH AFRICA:** Computing SA, Network World SA, Software World SA; **SPAIN:** Communicaciones World España, Computerworld España, Dealer World España, Macworld España, PC World España; **SRI LANKA:** Infolink PC World; **SWEDEN:** CAP&Design, Computer Sweden, Corporate Computing Sweden, Internetworld Sweden, it.branschen, Macworld Sweden, MaxiData Sweden, MikroDatorn, Nätverk & Kommunikation, PC World Sweden, PCaktiv, Windows World Sweden; **SWITZERLAND:** Computerworld Schweiz, Macworld Schweiz, PCtip; **TAIWAN:** Computerworld Taiwan, Macworld Taiwan, NEW ViSiON/Publish, PC World Taiwan, Windows World Taiwan; **THAILAND:** Publish in Asia, Thai Computerworld; **TURKEY:** Computerworld Turkiye, Macworld Turkiye, Network World Turkiye, PC World Turkiye; **UKRAINE:** Computerworld Kiev, Multimedia World Ukraine, PC World Ukraine; **UNITED KINGDOM:** Acorn User UK, Amiga Action UK, Amiga Computing UK, Apple Talk UK, Computing, Macworld, Parents and Computers UK, PC Advisor, PC Home, PSX Pro, The WEB; **UNITED STATES:** Cable in the Classroom, CIO Magazine, Computerworld, DOS World, Federal Computer Week, GamePro Magazine, InfoWorld, I-Way, Macworld, Network World, PC Games, PC World, Publish, Video Event, THE WEB Magazine, and WebMaster; online webzines: JavaWorld, NetscapeWorld, and SunWorld Online; **URUGUAY:** InfoWorld Uruguay; **VENEZUELA:** Computerworld Venezuela, PC World Venezuela; and **VIETNAM:** PC World Vietnam.                                                                                                                   5/7/98

# Dedication

To Alex.

# Author's Acknowledgments

I'd like to thank Margy Levine Young and John Levine for moral support and for getting me into this terrific business. And additional thanks are due to John, who lent me a laptop so I could go off on a little adventure and still finish this book.

Thanks are also due to former and current Acquisitions Editors Tammy Goldfeld and Gareth Hancock for offering me the opportunity to write this book, and to my agent, Matt Wagner at Waterside Productions, for hammering out the details.

I could never get my work done if it weren't for Matt (also known as "Honey") providing around-the-clock moral support and keeping the computers in such a state that I could actually get work done.

I'd also like to thank Shannon Ross for guiding this book through editing and production, Kathy Simpson for forcing me to fix my use of the word "setting," and Joe Jansen and Chris Collins for getting all my illustrations in order.

I'd also like to acknowledge TIAC and IECC, my almost flawless Internet and e-mail providers.

# Publisher's Acknowledgments

We're proud of this book; please register your comments through our IDG Books Worldwide Online Registration Form located at: http://my2cents.dummies.com.

Some of the people who helped bring this book to market include the following:

*Acquisitions, Development, and Editorial*

**Project Editor:** Shannon Ross

**Assistant Acquisitions Editor:** Gareth Hancock

**Copy Editors:** Joe Jansen, Kathy Simpson

**Technical Reviewer:** Jim McCarter

**Editorial Managers:** Kristin A. Cocks, Seta K. Frantz

**Editorial Assistants:** Chris H. Collins, Michael D. Sullivan

*Production*

**Project Coordinator:** Sherry Gomoll

**Layout and Graphics:** Brett Black, J. Tyler Connor, Angela F. Hunckler, Drew R. Moore, Anna Rohrer, Theresa Sánchez-Baker, Brent Savage

**Proofreaders:** Kelli Botta, Rachel Garvey, Nancy Price, Dwight Ramsey, Robert Springer, Carrie Voorhis, Karen York

**Indexer:** Sharon Hilgenberg

---

*General and Administrative*

**IDG Books Worldwide, Inc.:** John Kilcullen, CEO; Steven Berkowitz, President and Publisher

**IDG Books Technology Publishing:** Brenda McLaughlin, Senior Vice President and Group Publisher

**Dummies Technology Press and Dummies Editorial:** Diane Graves Steele, Vice President and Associate Publisher; Mary Bednarek, Director of Acquisitions and Product Development; Kristin A. Cocks, Editorial Director

**Dummies Trade Press:** Kathleen A. Welton, Vice President and Publisher; Kevin Thornton, Acquisitions Manager

**IDG Books Production for Dummies Press:** Michael R. Britton, Vice President of Production and Creative Services; Cindy L. Phipps, Manager of Project Coordination, Production Proofreading, and Indexing; Kathie S. Schutte, Supervisor of Page Layout; Shelley Lea, Supervisor of Graphics and Design; Debbie J. Gates, Production Systems Specialist; Robert Springer, Supervisor of Proofreading; Debbie Stailey, Special Projects Coordinator; Tony Augsburger, Supervisor of Reprints and Bluelines

**Dummies Packaging and Book Design:** Robin Seaman, Creative Director; Kavish + Kavish, Cover Design

◆

The publisher would like to give special thanks to Patrick J. McGovern, without whom this book would not have been possible.

◆

# Contents at a Glance

# Table of Contents

## Part IV: Queries: Getting Answers from Your Data ...... 79

# How to Use This Book

If you're looking for a book that fits neatly beside your monitor and gives you easy access to short and useful descriptions of how to get your work done, then this is the book for you. *Access 97 For Windows For Dummies Quick Reference* is a great book to have when all you want is a reference — not the nitty-gritty *why* and *why not.* This little book doesn't take up space telling you *why* you need to do something, but it's a great place to find out *how* to do a task.

In this book, you can find loads of step-by-step instructions organized alphabetically by topic. If you already know what you need to find, look it up alphabetically in the appropriate part. If you can't find what you need, check the Index or the Table of Contents. If you just want to know more about some aspect of Access, flip through a part or two and read the topics that look unfamiliar to you. You may discover tricks and tips you didn't even know existed!

This is not the book to use when you're building a database from scratch and you don't know where to start. For that situation, you need a more comprehensive book — one that shows you the ins and outs of building a new database. For such in-depth information, pick up a copy of *Access 97 For Windows For Dummies,* by John Kaufeld, or, for a more tutorial approach, *Dummies 101: Access 97 For Windows,* by Margy Levine Young.

# How This Book Is Organized

This book covers beginning and intermediate skills, and (to a lesser extent) advanced skills. You won't find hard-core Access programming stuff here, such as setting up menu-based MIS systems and programming Access using VBA. You *will* find specific instructions on how to get your daily work done in Access.

The book is broken into eight parts, each dealing with a specific aspect of Access:

## Part I: Access Basics

Part I introduces the basics — the things you really need to know before you can get much done in Access. Starting Access, closing Access, opening a database, using dialog boxes, and getting help are all covered in this part. You can also find information on the Access screen, how to work with windows, and some general pointers on using those wonderful Access wizards.

Part I is the only part that's not alphabetized. Instead, this part presents some basic Access 97 skills in a logical order. If you're looking for tips on getting started with Access 97, you may want to go through Part I from start to finish, just to get yourself headed in the right direction. Then you can use the rest of the book as an alphabetical reference.

## Part II: Creating and Navigating a Database

Part II covers the specifics of creating a new database and finding your way around a database that you already have. This part also covers how to delete and copy Access objects, such as tables and queries, and how to create relationships between fields in different tables.

## Part III: Tables: A Home for Your Data

Part III describes all the nitty-gritty tasks you need to know to create tables and put data into them. Turn to this part to find out how to define fields, enter and edit data, and work in the Table, Datasheet, and Design views. You may also discover more about data types and how to use input masks and validation rules to limit the data that you and others can enter in a field.

## Part IV: Queries: Getting Answers from Your Data

Part IV deals with all the details you need to know to use queries to get the answers you need from your data. Queries are great for displaying related information from different tables or for finding specific data that meets certain criteria you set. You can also use queries to create aggregate calculations: Want to know how many orders you receive in a week? A query can give you the answer.

## Part V: Reporting Results

Part V covers everything you need to know about reports. Reports are the best Access tool for putting your results on paper. Reports enable you to group and sort data.

You can create a report from a table or a group of tables. If you don't want to display every record in a report, you can create your report from a query that produces only the records you want to see, or you can work from a filtered table.

Most of the work you do on a report takes place in Report Design view. This part tells you how to use Report Design view to create sections in a report, put text and lines on the report, and display the contents of fields.

## Part VI: Forms for Displaying and Entering Data

Forms are a great way to enter data. They enable you to create on-screen something very like a paper form that you may use to record information with a pen. By using an Access form, you can display only relevant fields. You can even create check boxes and drop-down lists to ease data entry.

## Part VII: Printing Your Work for the World to See

You can print any object in an Access database. Whatever you print, this part arms you with the skills you need — such as how to preview before you print, how to change the page layout, and how to print only specific pages. This part also covers how to cancel a print job and how to fix the most common printer problems.

## Part VIII: Access 97 Tips and Tricks

This part contains some of the miscellaneous useful topics that don't fit into another part. In this part, you can find details on cutting and pasting, checking the spelling of your data, sharing your Access data, and using data stored in other applications. This part also contains a list of additional Access resources to turn to when you're stuck. The most important topic in this part is information about how to back up your database.

# Conventions Used in This book

The directions in this book often include a menu command. Such commands appear like this:

Choose File⇨Open.

This sentence tells you to click the File option on the main menu and then click Open from the drop-down menu.

You can also choose menu commands by using the *hotkeys,* the underlined letters in the command. First press the Alt key to make the menu active and then type the underlined letters to choose the menu item.

The directions in this book may also tell you to type something.

**Things you should type appear in bold.**

You may also run into messages that your computer is sending to you:

```
Computer messages look like this.
```

Occasionally, the text refers to a generic table or field name. The generic name will appear in italics. So if you see *TableName.* * in the book, you should look for the name of an actual table in your database, followed by a period and an asterisk on your screen.

# Icons Used in This Book

What's a computer book without icons to help show you the way? The following icons appear in this book:

This icon signals a good way to do something, often a method you may not have considered.

This icon flags the quickest way to complete a task.

This icon points out information about the latest piece of Microsoft hardware: the IntelliMouse.

This icon points out a feature that doesn't work exactly as you may expect it to.

This icon steers you clear of pitfalls that could be harmful to you, your computer, or your data.

This icon refers to another IDG Books Worldwide book for more information about the task at hand.

# *Send Me E-Mail*

Please let me know what you think of this book. Do you find it useful? Would you find it useful if only some particular topic were covered differently? I want to know — you can help me improve the next version!

To tell IDG Books Worldwide, Inc., (and me!) what you think of *Access 97 For Windows For Dummies Quick Reference,* complete and mail the card at the back of the book. Or, for the more cyberminded reader, you can go online to provide your feedback at http://www. dummies.com/comments.html. This Web site even gives you the opportunity to register to win another great ...*For Dummies* book!

For updates and more information about this book, visit http:// net.dummies.net/books. You can also send e-mail directly to me at accessQR@dummies.com, or snail mail (the kind that goes through the post office) to this address:

Alison Barrows
c/o IDG Books Worldwide, Inc.
919 E. Hillsdale Blvd., Suite 400
Foster City, CA 94404-9691

# Part 1

# Access Basics

Part I provides some basic database concepts as well as a quick overview of what you need to know about Windows 95 to use Access 97. This part covers some fundamental definitions, such as what a database is and what its most important pieces are. Look here for a review of the parts of the Access screen and for information on how to open, save, and close database files. This part also covers how to get online help, including how to use that cute little animated paper clip, the Office Assistant.

## In this part...

- ✓ **Defining a database**
- ✓ **Starting Access 97**
- ✓ **Naming the parts of the screen**
- ✓ **Using dialog boxes**
- ✓ **Working in the Windows 95 environment**
- ✓ **Opening, saving, and closing an Access file**
- ✓ **Getting online help**
- ✓ **Quitting Access 97**

# *About Databases*

A *database* is an organized collection of related data. In a well-built database, you can organize your data so that you see only the data you need to see, in the order you need to see it. In other words, a database enables you to *filter* and *sort* data. You can also choose the format in which you want to view your data — a table, for example, or a form.

On the most basic level, databases are organized into records. A *record* is one line of related information. If you think of your address book as a database, one record is the information about your best friend — her name, address, phone number, and any other information that you have about her in the address book.

You can organize information in a database into tables consisting of rows and columns. The rows are records, and the columns are fields. A *field* is one category of information that you collect for every record. In a database that stores your address book, the fields may be first name, last name, street address, birthday, and so on.

| Catalog | Address1 | Address2 | City | State | |
|---|---|---|---|---|---|
| Chadwick's | One Chadwick Pl. | Box 1600 | Brockton | MA | 02 |
| Coming Home | 1 Lands End Lane | | Dodgeville | WI | 53 |
| Country Curtains | At the Red Lion Inn | | Stockbridge | MA | 02 |
| Crate & Barrel | P.O. Box 9059 | | Wheeling | IL | 60 |
| Crate and Barrel | | | | | |
| Harry and David | P.O. Box 712 | | Medford | OR | 97 |
| hold everything | P.O. Box 7807 | | San Francisco | CA | 94 |
| Home Decorators C | | | | | |
| J. Crew | One Ivy Crescent | | Lynchburg | VA | 24 |
| JCPenney | P.O. Box 2021 | | Milwaukee | WI | 53 |
| L. L. Bean | | | Freeport | ME | 04 |

Record: 6 of 15

**Remember:** It's important to store each type of information in a separate field. Organizing your data into many different fields enables you to slice the data any way you want. If you decide that having separate fields for first and last names is a waste of time, you lose out on the option of sorting the database by either first or last name.

Access is a *relational database,* which means that one database file can consist of many tables of related data. For example, you may have a table that lists orders and includes the product number of each item ordered, and another table that contains information about products and that also includes the product number. Tables relate to each other when you use identical fields (in this case, product number) in more than one table and tell Access that the two fields are related. Thanks to the related fields, you can ask your database a question that requires it to use more than one table to answer.

An Access database can contain different types of Access *objects:* tables, forms, queries, and reports.

✦ Access stores data in *tables.*

✦ You use Access *forms* just like paper forms: to enter and display data.

✦ You create *queries* to gather the information you need about the data you've entered.

✦ Use *reports* to present the information you gather about your data.

# Starting Access 97

Windows 95 almost always gives you more than one way to perform a task, and starting Access is no exception. The most popular way to start Access is to use the Start button in the taskbar.

Here are some ways to start Access, including the Start-button method:

✦ Click the Start button and move the mouse pointer (the highlight moves with it) to the Programs option. Then click the Microsoft Access option. (You may have to highlight the Microsoft Office option in order to see and click Microsoft Access.)

✦ If you have the Microsoft Office shortcut bar, click the Open a Document button on it, choose an existing Access database, and click the Open button.

✦ Double-click an existing Access database file in Windows Explorer or My Computer. Windows 95 starts Access and opens the database that you double-clicked.

To read about more ways to open any Windows 95 program, get a book about Windows 95, such as Andy Rathbone's *Windows 95 For Dummies* (IDG Books Worldwide, Inc.).

# Touring the Database Window

When you use Access, you work with different types of database objects, such as the Database window (Mission Control for the database, if you like), tables, forms, queries, and reports. Each of these types of objects has its own tools. You see a different menu and toolbar, depending on which type of object you're working with.

Although the specific buttons and menu items may change, some parts of the screen remain the same:

Close
Maximize
Minimize
Toolbar
Menu
Title bars

**Microsoft Access**
File Edit View Insert Tools Window Help

**Catalog orders : Database**

| Tables | Queries | Forms | Reports | Macros | Modules | | Address1 |

Catalogs
Items ordered
Order Summary

Open
Design
New

e Chadwick Pl.
ands End Lane
the Red Lion Inn
). Box 9059
). Box 7807

e Ivy Crescent
). Box 2021

ands End Lane

Orvis    800-541-3541    540-313-7053    Distribution Center

Record: |◄ ◄| 1 |► ►| ►*| of 13

Ready    NUM

Status bar    Access windows    Scroll bars

You can find out what a button is called by placing the mouse pointer on it (don't click it, though). A ToolTip pops up to give you the button's name.

Some buttons have little arrows next to them; click the arrow to see several options. Each option on the drop-down list has an icon next to it.

The icon for one of the options on the drop-down list matches the icon on the button. Clicking the button performs the task listed next to the matching icon. The New Object button, shown above, creates an AutoForm — unless you use the drop-down list to choose another kind of object to create.

The Database window is the place where you can find all the components of your database. It looks like this:

| Catalog orders : Database | _ □ × |
| --- | --- |
| ⊞ Tables \| 🗗 Queries \| 📰 Forms \| 🗐 Reports \| 🗇 Macros \| 📇 Modules | |
| ⊞ Catalogs | <u>O</u>pen |
| 📇 Order Summary | <u>D</u>esign |
| ⊞ Orders by item | <u>N</u>ew |

To see the names of all the objects of a certain type, click the appropriate tab. To see the names of all the forms in the database, for example, click the Forms tab. To see a specific form, click the form name to select it and then click Open.

If you're viewing an object in the database and want to see the Database window, click the Database Window button on the toolbar.

The Office Assistant—a cute, animated paper clip that appears in its own window—pops up the first time you start Access 97.

*See also* "Getting Help," later in this part.

# Getting Around in Access 97

As with all Windows programs, Access 97 provides a host of ways to get you from point A to point B. You can use the mouse or the keyboard, you can use menus, dialog boxes, buttons, key combinations, and more.

## Using the mouse

Odds are that you can recognize your mouse, even at ten paces. Or perhaps you use a trackball, or another pointing device. The important thing is that you have a mouse (or other pointing device) and know how to use it. Otherwise, Access 97 (like any Windows 95 program) can be next to impossible to navigate.

The new Microsoft IntelliMouse gives you even more ways to navigate Access 97 windows than a regular mouse does. The IntelliMouse has a wheel between the two buttons. You can use the wheel to pan — hold the wheel down and move out of any window in Access that has a scroll bar, and Access shows you more of the window. You can also turn the wheel up or down to scroll up or down in any window that has a vertical scroll bar.

Your pointing device controls the pointer, which often looks like an arrow. The pointer can change shape, though, to indicate the kind of job that it's ready to do. You can see examples of other pointer shapes throughout this book. In general, when I tell you to *click* something, you should move the pointer to that thing and then click the left mouse button. When you need to use the right mouse button, I tell you to *right-click*.

Following are some common pointing procedures and how to perform them:

| What I Tell You to Do | How to Do It |
| --- | --- |
| Click something | Move the pointer to the something and click the left mouse button. |
| Double-click something | Move the pointer to the something and click the left mouse button twice, quickly, without moving the pointer even the littlest bit. |
| Right-click something | Move the pointer to the something and click the right mouse button. |
| Click and drag | Click the something (use the left mouse button), hold the mouse button down, and move the mouse without letting go of the button. |
| Shift+click | Press and hold down the Shift key while you click the left mouse button. |
| Ctrl+click | Press and hold down the Ctrl key while you click the left mouse button. |

## Using the keyboard

A computer's keyboard looks much like the keyboard on a typewriter, but a computer keyboard has some additional keys that don't exist on a typewriter. The following table lists those special keys, which you may need to use with Access 97. Some of the following descriptions are a little vague because, depending on what kind of object you're working with (a form, report, or table, for example), a particular key may work differently.

| Key | What It Does |
| --- | --- |
| Esc | The "yikes" key, Esc backs you out of menu commands and cancels dialog boxes. Esc is a good key to press if you don't like what's happening on your screen. |
| Function keys (F1 through F12 or so) | These keys are assigned to menu commands. |
| Delete | This key deletes the selected characters or deletes the character to the right of the cursor. |

| Key | What It Does |
|---|---|
| Home | Used for navigation, this key often moves you to the beginning of whatever you're looking at. In a table, pressing the Home key moves you to the beginning of a row. |
| End | Used for navigation, this key often moves you to the end of whatever you're looking at. In a table, pressing the End key moves you to the end of a row. |
| Insert | This key toggles between insert and overstrike mode when you're editing. *Insert* means that new characters you type are inserted where the cursor is, and the existing characters move to make space. *Overstrike* means that each character you type replaces the character following the cursor. When you're in overstrike mode, you see OVR in the status bar. |
| PgUp | Used for navigation, this key usually moves you up one screen of data. |
| PgDn | Used for navigation, this key usually moves you down one screen of data. |
| Arrow keys without numbers | Also called *cursor control keys*. Used for navigation, these keys enable you to move up, down, left, and right one character or one unit at a time. |
| Arrow keys with numbers | These keys work like arrow keys without numbers when Num Lock is off; they enter numbers when Num Lock is on. |
| Numeric keypad | The keys in this keypad enter numbers when Num Lock is on; otherwise, they work like arrow keys without numbers. |
| Num Lock | This key turns Num Lock *(number lock)* on and off. |

## *Working with windows*

When you use Windows 95 programs, you can choose how much space the program's window occupies on-screen — the entire screen, part of the screen, or just a button in the taskbar. Some programs, including Access, display windows within the program window. The three buttons in the top-right corner of a window control the way that the window appears. Here's how to tell a window how much space to take up:

+ Click the Minimize button to make the window only a button in the taskbar. (Click the appropriate button in the taskbar to see the window again.)

+ Click the Maximize button to make the window take up the entire screen.

+ Click the Restore button to make the window take up only part of the screen. When the window is *restored* (that is, taking up only part of the screen), you can size and move it.

- Move any window by clicking and dragging its title bar.

- Resize a window by moving the pointer to the edge of the window, where it turns into a double-headed arrow; then click and drag the border to make the window a different size.

You can use all these tricks on other Access windows, too. For example, when you see a list of fields in the Report or Form Design view, they appear in their own window — you can move or resize the window using the click-and-drag techniques.

## Handling dialog boxes

Dialog boxes enable you to tell Access what you want it to do. Don't be daunted when you see many settings in a dialog box. Often, all you need to do is find the setting that you know you need to change and leave the rest alone.

You need to know how to use all kinds of dialog-box settings. Here's the roundup of all the types of settings and how they work:

| Setting | How to Use It |
| --- | --- |
| Check boxes | Click the box to turn the setting off and on. The setting is on when the check mark appears. |
| Scroll lists | Click the arrows to change the setting, or select the contents and type the new value. |
| Radio buttons | Click an option to move the setting. You can select only one setting in the group at a time. |

| Setting | How to Use It |
|---|---|
| Drop-down lists | Click the setting or the arrow next to the list box to display the options. Click the option you want. |
| Buttons | Click a button to execute an action or display another dialog box. (Buttons labeled with an ellipsis display another dialog box.) |
| Sample boxes | Look here to see what the option you select will look like. |
| Tabs | Click a tab to display a different group of options. |
| Settings to type | Type text or values in these boxes. |

You can move from one setting to another in a dialog box by using the mouse to click the setting you want to use or by pressing Alt and the setting's hot key (the underlined letter). But the fastest way to move to the next setting in a dialog box is to press Tab.

# Opening a Database File

You must save your database files if you want to use them again. An Access database file consists of the data you've entered into it and the different objects (tables, queries, forms, and reports) that you've defined. Access databases have the extension .mdb, and are stored in the My Documents folder on your hard disk, unless you specify a different folder in which to store them. To work on a database, you have to open its database file.

You can open a database file after you've started Access, or you can just open an Access file — by opening it, you also start Access.

When you start Access, you see a dialog box that lists databases that you've used recently. To open a database, select it from this initial dialog box ( be sure that the Open an Existing Database option is selected), and click OK.

If you're already in Access, you need to use the Open dialog box to open a file, or choose a recently used database file from the bottom of the File menu.

Follow these steps to use the Open dialog box to open a database:

*1.* Click the Open button. (Alternatively, choose File⇨Open or press Ctrl+O.)

Another way to display the Open dialog box is to select the More Files option on the dialog box that appears when you first start Access, and then click OK.

| Open | ? X |
|---|---|
| Look in: 🗀 My Documents | 🖃 🔁 🔍 🔃 🗐 ▦ ▦ ▦ 🗐 |

| | |
|---|---|
| 📄 1995 Orders.mdb | Open |
| 📄 Animal Hospital.mdb | Cancel |
| 📄 Catalog Orders.mdb | Advanced... |
| 📄 Shortcut to Northwind | |
| 📄 Test.mdb | ☐ Exclusive |
| 📄 Time and Billing1.mdb | |
| 📄 WORKOUT1.mdb | |
| 📄 Yoga Classes.mdb | |

Find files that match these search criteria:

| File name: | ▾ | Text or property: | ▾ | Find Now |
|---|---|---|---|---|
| Files of type: Microsoft Access Databases (*.mdb) ▾ | | Last modified: any time ▾ | | New Search |

8 file(s) found.

*2.* Select the file that you want.

*3.* Click the Open button or simply double-click the filename.

Access opens the database.

Make sure that the Files of Type list box shows Microsoft Access Databases (*.mdb) or All Files (*.*). The Files of Type setting limits the files that appear in the Open dialog box, so if another option is selected, you won't see Access database files.

If you recently used the Access database file that you want to use now, you can start Access and open the database by choosing the file from the Documents menu. The Documents option in the Start menu also lists the last few files that you used. Click the Windows 95 Start button, choose Documents, and click the file you want to open.

# Saving a Database File

Access is designed so that many people can use one database — and all at the same time, if they need to. So, unlike a spreadsheet or word processing program, Access doesn't require you to save the entire file at the same time. Instead, you save one object definition (such as a table, form, or query) at a time, and Access updates the database file accordingly. Access saves new data to the database file as soon as you move to the next cell in a form or table.

 To save an object definition, make the object active (by clicking in its window) and then click the Save button on the toolbar, press Ctrl+S, or choose File➪Save. If you close an object without saving it, Access displays a dialog box asking whether you want to save the object:

+ Click Yes to save the object.

+ Click No to close the object without saving changes to the definition.

+ Click Cancel to cancel the command to close the object.

# Closing a Database File

To close a database, simply close the database window — the one that has `Name of the database file: Database` in the title bar. To close the window, first make it active by clicking it (the title bar is a good place to click). Then choose one of the following methods:

 + Click the Close button in the upper-right corner.

+ Click the properties box in the upper-left corner of the window and then choose Close (or double-click the control-box menu).

+ Press Ctrl+F4.

# Working with Wizards

Access provides wizards to help you build and use databases. *Wizards* consist of a series of dialog boxes that ask you questions and then create something (such as a database, a query, or a report) based on your answers. The many wizards in Access 97 do a variety of tasks, but they all work in a similar way: They present you with screens that ask you questions, such as which tables or fields you want to use or which format you prefer.

I cover specific wizards in other parts of this book, but the following sections cover basic techniques you must know in order to use any wizard.

## Selecting fields

Many wizards have windows like the following one, where you choose fields.

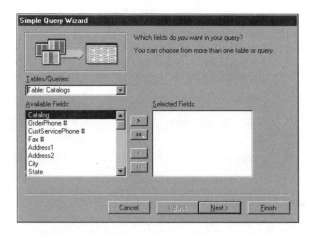

To tell Access that you want to use a field, you first have to tell it where the field is coming from by choosing a table or query from the drop-down list in the Tables/Queries list box. Access displays the fields from the table or query you've chosen in the Available Fields list box. Use one of the following methods to tell Access that you want it to use a field:

> ✦ Double-click it.

> ✦ Select it and click the single right-facing arrow button.

To choose all the fields displayed in the Available Fields list box, click the double right-facing arrow.

If you make a mistake, and want to remove a field from the Selected Fields list box, double-click it, or select it and click the single left-facing arrow button.

To remove all fields from the Selected Fields list box, click the double left-facing arrow button.

To select fields from other tables or queries, choose another table or query from the Tables/Queries drop-down list and select the additional fields.

## Viewing more windows

When you've answered all the questions on one window of a wizard, you're ready to see the next. The buttons at the bottom of the wizard enable you to proceed through the questions the wizard asks you:

- **Cancel:** Exits the wizard without letting the wizard complete its task

- **Back:** Displays the previous window of the wizard

- **Next:** Displays the next window of the wizard

- **Finish:** Tells Access to complete whatever it is that this particular wizard does, using the information you've given it

Any wizard has information that it needs in order to work, and other settings that are optional (if you don't change them, Access uses a default value). After you give a wizard the information it needs, the Finish button becomes clickable. You can click the Finish button to tell the wizard to complete its task, or you can click the Next button to see more settings. If you click Finish, the wizard uses the default values on any windows that you chose not to view.

When you get to the last window of a wizard, you see the black and white checkered Finish flag. Access asks you if you want help displayed, and it often asks you to name the object the wizard is creating and choose how you want to view the new object. After you finish with these settings, click the Finish button to tell the wizard to complete its task.

# Getting Help

Access offers you help in several ways. You can use the Office Assistant or the old-fashioned online Help system, for example. Both methods tap into the same information; the difference is in the way you find the information. You may want the more advanced help offered by the Developers Solutions database.

## Online help

To get online help, choose Help⇨Contents and Index. Access displays the Help Topics window, with the Contents or the Index tab selected.

Tabs

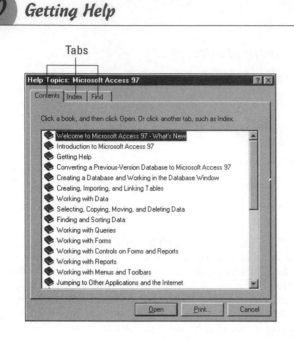

The Help Topics window has three tabs that guide you to the
different types of help that you may need:

✦ **Contents:** Displays a list of help topics (like a manual). Double-
click topics that have a book in front of them to display subtopics. Double-click topics that have a question mark to display an
actual help screen.

✦ **Index:** Displays an index of topics covered in the Help system.
Type the first few letters of the topic that you're looking for in
the first box. Choose the topic you want to view by double-
clicking it or by selecting it and then clicking the Display button.

✦ **Find:** Displays an index of words used in the Help system. Type
the word that you want to find in the first box. The second box
suggests topics that you may be looking for. Select a topic by
clicking it; then choose a help topic in the third box. Display the
Help window by double-clicking the topic or by selecting it and
then clicking the Display button.

The first time you use the Find tab, Access asks you what size Help
database you want to create. Use the recommended Minimum size
unless you have a specific reason to choose the Maximum size.
(Create the maximum-size database only if you have scads of space
on your hard disk.)

The Help window also provides some tools that you can use: buttons,
links, and windows that pop up when you click particular words or
symbols.

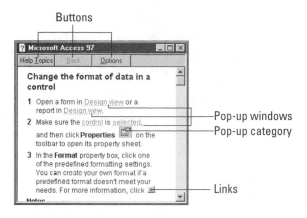

Buttons

Pop-up windows
Pop-up category
Links

The buttons at the top of the Help window are useful for navigating the Help system and working with the help you find:

+ **Help Topics button:** Displays the Help Topics window (the one with the Contents, Index, and Find tabs)

+ **Back button:** Displays the last Help window that you saw

+ **Options button:** Displays a drop-down list of options — things that you can do with Help windows

Another kind of Help window, sometimes called *Large Card Help,* gives you overviews of topics. The subtopics of the *Introduction to Microsoft Access 97* topic in the Contents tab are Large Card Help windows.

Click for more help    Click here to display pop-up windows

```
Microsoft Access 97
Help Topics   Back   Options
1 2 3

Tables: What they are and how they work

A table is a collection of
data about a specific topic,
such as products or suppliers.    Fields    Suppliers : Table
Using a separate table for              Supplier ID   Company Name
each topic means you store                    1   Exotic Liquids
that data only once, which                    2   New Orleans Cajun Delights
makes your database                           3   Grandma Kelly's Homestead
more efficient and reduces                    4   Tokyo Traders
data-entry errors. Tables
organize data into          Products : Table
columns (called fields)       Product Name  Supplier ID   Units In Stock
and rows (called records).    Chai              1              39
                              Chang             1              17
                              Aniseed Syrup     1              13
            Records          Carnarvon Tigers   2              53

                                  A common field relates two tables
```

Click here to display pop-up windows

Close Help windows by clicking their Close buttons.

Unless you've changed the default setting, when you press F1, the Office Assistant appears. If you find the Office Assistant a little annoying and prefer to see the Help Topics window when you press F1, follow these steps:

*1.* Press F1 or click the Office Assistant button in the toolbar to display the Office Assistant and its dialog-box thingy. If the Office Assistant is already visible, click it to display the dialog box.

Access displays the Office Assistant dialog box.

*2.* Click Options.

*3.* Click the Respond to F1 key option (the first setting on the Options tab) to remove the check mark from the check box.

*4.* Choose OK to exit the dialog box.

## *The Office Assistant*

Access 97 practically attacks you with a new kind of help in the form of the Office Assistant, an animated paper clip that appears in its own window. When the Office Assistant is on-screen, it replaces dialog boxes that would otherwise appear on-screen and amuses you with animation when the computer is doing something (such as saving a file).

The Office Assistant gives you help by allowing you to type a question using plain, old English.

Here's how to work with the Office Assistant:

✦ You can close the Office Assistant by clicking its Close button.

✦ If you've closed the Office Assistant and want it back, click the Office Assistant button on the toolbar or anywhere else you see it (it appears in some dialog boxes), or press F1.

✦ If you want help, click the Office Assistant; type your question in the white box; and then press Enter or click Search. The Office Assistant suggests some topics that may be what you're looking for. Click the topic or the blue dot next to the topic to display the help window on the topic.

✦ Choose a different Office Assistant (it doesn't have to look like a paper clip — it can be a bouncing smiley face or a cat made out of notebook paper, among other choices) by clicking the Office Assistant, choosing Options, clicking the Gallery tab (or by right-clicking the Office Assistant and choosing Choose Assistant), and following the directions in the dialog box.

✦ Change the way the Office Assistant works by clicking it, choosing Options, and changing settings in the Options tab. The settings let you tell the Office Assistant the kind of help you want to see.

✦ View a tip by clicking the Office Assistant and choosing Tips.

✦ Size the Office Assistant window by clicking and dragging the window border. You may want to make the Office Assistant smaller, so that it takes up less of the screen. The Office Assistant actually only has two sizes, so your choices here are limited. But when you click and drag the window border, you can change the size — it's just that you only have one choice.

✦ Move the Office Assistant out of the way by clicking and dragging the title bar.

## Sample databases

If you're building a database, Access comes with a couple of sample databases (Northwind and Developer Solutions) that can help you understand how Access databases work.

The Northwind database is a sample database that tracks products, suppliers, and sales for a company called Northwind Traders. Playing around with the Northwind database is one way to become familiar with different Access features.

The Northwind database is stored in C:\Program Files\Microsoft Office\Office\Samples\Northwind.mdb. But Access provides a shortcut to the Northwind database in the My Documents folder, which is the folder you usually see when you display the Open dialog box.

The Developer Solutions database is a self-documented database that provides help in building a database for intermediate and advanced users. *Self-documented* means that every feature used in the database is also explained, which is useful when you're trying to figure out how to use a feature that is used in the sample database.

You must install the Developer Solutions database in order to use it. By default, the file is stored in C:\Program Files\Microsoft Office\Office\Samples\Solutions.mdb.

***See also*** "Using other Access Resources," in Part VIII.

# *Quitting Access 97*

You quit Access the same way that you quit any other Windows 95 program. Once again, Windows 95 offers a boatload of options. If you have parts of a database open, and you've made changes since the last time you saved the object, Access gives you the option of saving the object before you quit.

Here are the most popular ways to close Access:

✦ Click the Close button in the top-right corner of the Access window (it looks like an X).

✦ Double-click the properties box in the top-left corner of the Access window. (Alternatively, click the properties box and then choose Close from the drop-down menu.)

✦ Choose File➪Exit from the Access menu.

✦ Press Alt+F4 when Access is the active window.

# Part II

# Creating and Navigating a Database

You can choose between two approaches to create a new database — you can start from scratch, or you can use a wizard. This part covers both methods.

After you create a database, or when you need to use one that someone else created, you have to know how to get around it — and that means knowing how to use the Database window.

## In this part . . .

- ✔ **Creating a database from scratch**
- ✔ **Using a wizard to create a database**
- ✔ **Using the Database window**
- ✔ **Navigating your database**
- ✔ **Creating relationships between tables**

# Creating a Database

Designing databases is a topic unto itself — this little Quick Reference certainly can't tell you everything you need to know. For more guidance on how to design a database, see *Access 97 For Windows For Dummies* by John Kaufeld (IDG Books Worldwide, Inc.).

Follow these general steps to create a database:

*1.* Open a new database.

*2.* Create tables. Design your tables so that as little information as possible is repeated.

*3.* Tell Access how your tables are related.

*4.* (Optional) Create forms to make data entry clearer and to display a full record's worth of information at a time.

*5.* Enter your data.

*6.* Create queries to give you the information you need.

*7.* Create reports to transfer the information to paper in a clear format.

## Creating a database from scratch

You can create an empty database in the following ways:

✦ If Access is closed, start it and, in the introductory dialog box, choose Blank Database. Access displays the File New Database dialog box, where you name the new database.

✦ When Access is closed, choose Open Office Document from the Windows 95 Start button menu (or click the New Office Document button in the Microsoft Office shortcut bar). You see the New Office Document dialog box with ten tabs at the top. Click the General tab, select the Blank Database icon, and click OK.

✦ If Access is running, click the New Database button, press Alt+N, or choose File⇨New Database. The New dialog box appears. Click the General tab in the New dialog box, select Blank Database, and then click OK. Access displays the File New Database dialog box.

To create a new database, you first have to give the database a filename. When you create a new database, Access displays the File New Database dialog box, with the File name setting highlighted. Type the name of the new database into the File name box. If you want to store the file in a folder other than the one displayed in the Save in setting, change the folder. Then click Create.

Access takes a few seconds to create the new database; then it displays the Tables tab of the Database window and the Database toolbar.

After you open a blank database, you need to create one or more tables to hold your data. You may also want to create forms to make entering your data easier. If you have more than one table, and they have related fields, you should define the relationships between the tables. Then you're ready to create queries and reports.

*See also* "Relating (Linking) Tables," in this part.

## Creating a database with a wizard

 Wizards are a great way to get a jumpstart on creating a database. Even if they don't provide exactly what you want, wizards give you a framework to start from.

*See also* "Working with Wizards," in Part I.

Access 97 comes with a number of database wizards:

| | |
|---|---|
| Address Book | Music Collection |
| Asset Tracking | Order Entry |
| Book Collection | Picture Library |
| Contact Management | Recipes |
| Donations | Resource Scheduling |
| Event Management | Service Call Management |
| Expenses | Students and Classes |
| Household Inventory | Time and Billing |
| Inventory Control | Video Collection |
| Ledger | Wine List |
| Membership | Workout |

Here's how to create a database by using a wizard:

**1.** Display the New dialog box by choosing <u>D</u>atabase Wizard in the initial screen when you open Access and clicking OK, choosing <u>F</u>ile⇨<u>N</u>ew from the menu, clicking the New File button, or pressing Ctrl+N.

Access displays the New dialog box.

**2.** Click the Databases tab.

You see a list of wizards. The name of the wizard gives you a general idea about what kind of data the wizard is set up to work with.

**3.** Click a database name to get a graphical overview of the wizard.

**4.** To open a wizard, double-click the database icon (or name), or click the icon once to select it and then click the OK button.

Access displays the File New Database dialog box where you can name the database.

**5.** Accept the name in the File name box by pressing Enter, or edit the name and press Enter.

**6.** The wizard takes a few moments to set up and then displays the first window, which shows you some information about the database that you're setting up. Click <u>N</u>ext to display the next window of the wizard.

Click the <u>F</u>inish button now to accept the wizard's defaults and create the database.

**7.** Use the options on each window of the wizard to customize the database the wizard is creating for you. You may see more than one screen of options. Follow the directions in each screen to determine which options to change. Access allows you to add additional fields, choose a form style, choose a report style, and give the database a name that will appear in the Access title bar. The last screen gives you a setting to check if you want to view online help about the database.

**8.** Click the <u>F</u>inish button to tell the wizard to create the database.

Finally, the database opens, displaying the Main Switchboard — a menu of options.

**9.** You can work with the database by using the menu, or you can display the familiar Database window by clicking the Database Window button. Redisplay the Main Switchboard by choosing it from the <u>W</u>indow menu. You can also view the Switchboard by clicking the Forms tab in the Database window and double-clicking Switchboard.

# Finding Your Way Around a Database

A database consists of objects. Tables, reports, forms, and queries are the types of objects that you're most likely to work with. You may also work with macros and modules.

You have to view an object before you can work with it. Think of the Database window as the Table of Contents for your database. From the Database window, you can tell Access which object you want to work with.

Tabs for each type of object in the database

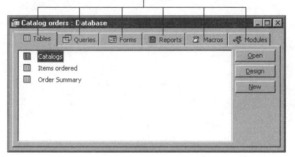

Here are some ways to view the database window:

◆ Click the Database Window button.

◆ Choose <u>W</u>indow from the menu and choose the item at the bottom of the drop-down menu that shows *Name of Database:* Database.

◆ If you can see even part of the Database window, you can click it to make it the active window.

When you can see the Database window, click any tab to see all the objects of that type. Click the Reports tab, for example, to see all the reports in the database. You can then use the <u>O</u>pen and <u>D</u>esign buttons (or the <u>P</u>review and <u>D</u>esign buttons) in the Database window to view the selected object, as follows:

**1.** Click the object that you want to work with.

**2.** Click <u>O</u>pen or <u>P</u>review to view the object, or click <u>D</u>esign to see the object in Design view. (Design view enables you to change the definition of the object. *See also* Parts III, IV, V, and VI for more information about using Design view for tables, queries, reports, and forms.)

## The Database window toolbar

The Database window contains some buttons that are useful for copying, printing, and creating objects. Here's the rundown on buttons you may find useful:

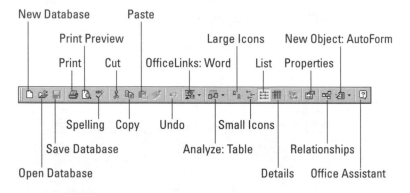

| Button | What It Does |
|---|---|
| New Database | Creates a new database |
| Open Database | Opens an existing database (and closes the open database) |
| Save Database | Saves the open database |
| Print | Prints the selected object |
| Print Preview | Displays the selected object as it looks when it's printed |
| Spelling | Checks the spelling of the selected object |
| Cut | Deletes the selected object and saves a copy in the Windows Clipboard |
| Copy | Copies the selected object to the Windows Clipboard |
| Paste | Pastes the contents of the Windows Clipboard to the Database window |
| Undo | Undoes the last undoable action |
| OfficeLinks | Opens another Office 97 application |
| Analyze | Runs the Table Analyzer Wizard or another analyzer wizard |
| Large Icons | Displays objects in the Database window as large icons |
| Small Icons | Displays objects in the Database window as small icons |
| List | Displays objects in the Database window in a list |
| Details | Displays objects in the Database window with details, including a description, last date modified, date created, and type of object |
| Properties | Displays the properties of the selected object |
| Relationships | Displays the Relationships window |

| Button | What It Does |
|---|---|
| New Object | Creates a new object |
| Office Assistant | Displays the Office Assistant |

## Changing the size of listed objects

You can choose how you want objects to appear in the Database window: as large icons, as small icons, in a list, or with details. Use toolbar buttons or the View menu to change the way that the objects are displayed.

**TIP**

One advantage of using Details view is that you can see when an object was last modified. You can also sort objects when you view them in Detail view — just click the gray column header to sort by that column. If you want to see which table was modified most recently, for example, click the Modified column header.

Column headers

| Name | Description | Modified | Created | Type |
|---|---|---|---|---|
| Catalogs | | 9/13/96 4:30:26 PM | 9/10/96 12:46:30 ... | Table |
| Items ordered | | 9/16/96 4:58:20 PM | 9/10/96 5:07:10 PM | Table |
| Order Summary | | 9/14/96 3:26:33 PM | 9/10/96 5:05:39 PM | Table |

## Changing the name of an object

You can change the name of any object in a database using the same method that you use to change the name of a Windows 95 file in My Computer or Explorer:

*1.* In the Database window, click the name of the object once to select it.

*2.* Click the object name a second time to edit it.

(Note that this is not the same as double-clicking the object, which opens the object. A good way to insure that you do not double-click is to move the mouse slightly between the two clicks.)

Access displays the object name with a box around it.

3. Initially, the name is selected — you can type a new name to replace the current name. Or you can use a cursor control key (also called an *arrow key*) to display the cursor, and then edit the name.

4. Press Enter to accept the new name. (Press Esc if you decide not to change the name of the object, after all.)

## Deleting an object

When you delete an object, you delete the object definition. In the case of a table, you also delete the data stored in the table.

To delete an object, select it in the Database window and press Del. Access displays a warning, giving you the chance to change your mind. Click Yes to delete the object.

You cannot undo the deletion of a database object.

## Copying objects

Occasionally, you may want to copy an object — perhaps you want to create a similar object, and copying and editing the original is more convenient that starting from scratch. Or maybe you want to create a backup before making significant changes.

You can copy an object using the Copy and Paste buttons:

1. Select the object in the Database window.

2. Click the Copy button.

3. Click the Paste button.

Access displays a version of the Paste dialog box (the version you see depends on the type of object you are copying).

4. Type a name for the copied object and, if necessary, change any settings that appear on the dialog box.

## Using Access windows

Only one window within Access can be active at a time. The *active window* is the window that you're working in — when you type or choose menu commands, the changes are reflected in the active window. The active window appears on top of any other windows, and its title bar is the same color as the Access title bar.

You can make a window active by:

✦ **Clicking it:** Often, you can see part of a window below other windows. Click any part of a window to make it active.

✦ **Using the Window menu:** The open windows are listed at the bottom of the menu; choose one to make it the active window.

# Relating (Linking) Tables

If your database consists of more than one table, you can't do much with the database as a whole (such as creating a query that needs more than one table to come up with an answer) until you tell Access how your tables are related. Telling Access about the relationships between tables is the key to making your relational database useful.

Pick your linked fields carefully — they should contain exactly the same concept in the two different tables. Usually, a linked field is the primary key in one table and simply information in the other table. A *primary key* is the field that uniquely identifies each record in the table.

***See also*** "Identifying Records with a Primary Key," in Part III, for more information about key fields.

If you're creating a database, it's quite appropriate (and necessary) to link tables. If you are not the creator of the database, however, you should consult an expert before changing any relationships that the creator defined.

Fields that appear in more than one table can be related in one of four ways. The four types of relationships are

♦ **One-to-one:** One record in one table has exactly one related record in another table. For example, each record in a table that lists employees by name has exactly one related record in a table that lists employees by employee number, and each employee number refers to only one employee.

♦ **One-to-many:** One record in the first table has many related records in the second table. For example, one table that lists artists may have many related records in another table that lists CDs by artist.

♦ **Many-to-one:** This relationship is identical to one-to-many, except that you look at the relationship from the other side. For example, each record in a table that lists CDs by artist has only one related record in a table that lists artists, but many CDs may have the same artist.

✦ **Many-to-many:** This relationship is the most complicated type. A many-to-many relationship requires a linking table. For example, the item field in a table listing items by the stores that sell them has a many-to-many relationship to the item field in a table listing stores and the items they sell. An item may be sold by many stores, and many stores sell a particular item.

To define the relationships in your database:

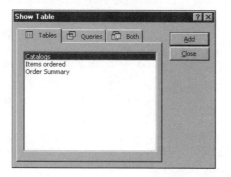

*1.* Choose Tools⇨Relationships or click the Relationships button on the toolbar.

If no relationships are defined in the database, Access displays the Show Table dialog box, where you indicate which tables will be involved in relationships. If you already have relationships defined in the database, Access displays the Relationships window. If you choose to, you can display the Show Table dialog box by clicking the Show Table button on the toolbar.

*2.* Add tables to the Relationships window by selecting them in the Show Table dialog box and clicking the Add button.

You can also add a table to the Relationships window by double-clicking the table name. You can select more than one table by selecting the first table and Ctrl+clicking the others. Then click the Add button.

*3.* Click the Close button to close the Show Table dialog box. If you need to display it again, click the Show Tables button on the toolbar.

*4.* Pick two related fields. Use the scroll bars to display the fields you want to link.

You can also use the new IntelliMouse wheel to scroll through each table until you see the related fields. *See* "Getting Around in Access 97," in Part I.

**5.** Drag the field from one table and drop it on the related field in the second table.

If you drag the wrong field, just drop it on the gray background rather than dragging it to a field in a table. Then you're ready to start again.

When you release the mouse button, Access displays the Relationships dialog box that details the nature of the relationship.

**6.** Make sure that the table and field names are correct; then click Create to tell Access to create the relationship.

If a field name is incorrect, you can change it by clicking the name of the field, clicking the arrow to display the drop-down list, and choosing another field name from the same table. If the relationship looks completely wrong, click Cancel.

To redisplay the Relationships dialog box after you have closed it, double-click the line joining two fields in the Relationships window.

**7.** Repeat Steps 4 through 6 to create relationships between other fields.

Access automatically saves the relationships that you create. You can view the relationships in the Relationships window.

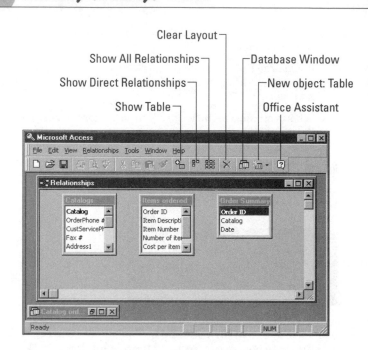

Clear Layout ⌐

Show All Relationships ⌐ ⌐Database Window

Show Direct Relationships ⌐ ⌐New object: Table

Show Table ⌐ Office Assistant

You may want to use the Enforce Referential Integrity check box on the Relationships dialog box to help you avoid "orphan" data. In the case of the Relationship pictured, an orphan record would be one in the Items Ordered table that had a value in the Order ID field that didn't have a matching value in the Order ID field of the Order Summary table. In the example database, that would mean that there was an item ordered without information entered detailing where the item was ordered from. When the Enforce Referential Integrity check box contains a check mark, Access adds symbols to the line representing the link to show the "one" and "many" sides of the relationship.

To delete a relationship, click the line that connects two fields and press Delete.

TIP ✦ You can move tables around in the Relationships window so that the relationships are easy to understand; just drag the title bar of the table to move it. You can also size a table so that you can see more field names; just drag the border.

# Part III

# Tables: A Home for Your Data

*Tables* are the basic building blocks of a database — they hold the raw data in the database. Forms, queries, and reports are all dependent on the data in the tables and the relationships defined between fields.

To create a useful database, you must first design your tables and fill them with data. This part contains all the information you need to know about tables and the data that goes in them — from creating a table with the Table Wizard to using a table to screen your data before you enter it into the database.

## In this part . . .

- ✓ **Creating a table in Design view**
- ✓ **Creating a table in Datasheet view**
- ✓ **Creating a table with the Table Wizard**
- ✓ **Masking out incorrect data**
- ✓ **Entering data into a table**
- ✓ **Finding data in a table**
- ✓ **Defining and formatting fields**
- ✓ **Sorting and filtering tables**

# About Tables

You can work with tables in two different views: Datasheet view and Design view.

## Working in Datasheet view

A table in Datasheet view looks like a spreadsheet — it stores a collection of similar data in records and fields. As in a spreadsheet, *records* store information for an item; *fields* define the type of information that is stored for each item.

To display a table in Datasheet view:

✦ Double-click the name of the table in the Datasheet window.

✦ Select the table in the datasheet window and click <u>O</u>pen.

 ✦ Click the Datasheet View button when the table is in Design view.

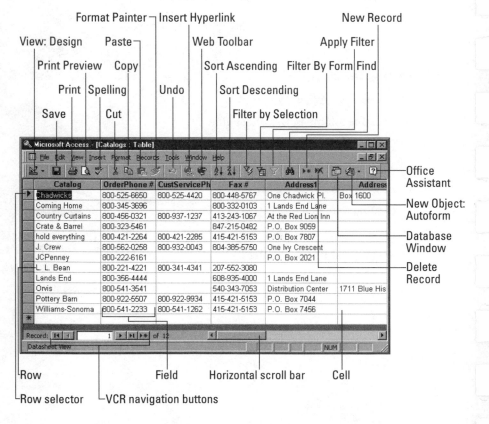

## Working in Design view

Design view gives you ways to control the table. You use Design view to define the type of data stored in a field, define the format of a field, identify the primary key, and enter data validation rules.

To display a table in Design view:

✦ Hold down the Ctrl key while you double-click the name of the table in the Datasheet window.

✦ Select the table in the datasheet window and click <u>D</u>esign.

 ✦ Click the Design View button when the table is in Datasheet view.

View: Datasheet   Copy ┌Paste   Insert Rows

   Print Preview │ Format Painter ┌ Delete Rows

   Save │ Spelling │ Primary Key │ Properties

   Print │ Cut │ Undo │ Indexes │ Build ┌Database Window

                     —Office Assistant

                     —New Object: Autoform

└Primary key   Field Properties   Selected row

└Row selector

In Design view, each field gets a row, with the field name displayed in the first column, the type of data stored in the field displayed in the second column, and a description of the field displayed in the third column.

The bottom half of the Design view window is called the Field Properties pane, and it displays additional options for the selected field (the one with a triangle in the row selector, immediately to the left of the field name). **See also** "Customizing Fields Using the Field Properties Pane," later in this part.

# Adding Data to Your Database

The easiest way put data into a database, or to work with the data that's already there, is to use Datasheet view.

*See* "Creating a New Table," in this part, if you haven't yet created a table to which you can add data. *See also* "About Tables," for a picture of the Datasheet view with all its various parts labeled.

Here's how to add new records to an already existing table:

*1.* Open the table to which you want to add data.

The easiest way to open a table is to double-click the table name in the Database window.

 *2.* Click the New Record button on the toolbar or at the bottom of the datasheet window.

Access moves the cursor to the last record, which is blank and waiting for input.

*3.* Type the appropriate information in the first field.

*4.* Press Enter or Tab after you type the data in a cell to move to the next field. You can also click a cell to move the cursor.

*5.* Enter data in all the fields in the record (as needed) by repeating Steps 3 and 4. To enter data for another record, simply press Enter when the cursor is in the last field — Access automatically creates a new record.

 Access automatically saves the data in the database file when you move to the next cell.

# Blocking Unwanted Data with an Input Mask

An *input mask* limits the information that's allowed in a field. Use an input mask with a validation rule to protect a field from data that is incorrect or that just doesn't belong there. *See also* "Limiting Data Entries with a Validation Rule," later in this part.

To use an input mask, enter a series of characters in the Input Mask section of the Field Properties pane to tell Access what kind of data to expect. Data that doesn't match the input mask cannot be entered. You can create input masks for text, number, and currency data; other data types don't have the Input Mask field property.

You can use an input mask to specify that the first character must be a letter, and every character after the first, a number, for example. You can also use an input mask to add characters to a field — for example, use an input mask to display ten digits as a phone number, with parentheses around the first three digits and a dash after the sixth digit. If the data in a field varies or is not easily described, it's probably not a good candidate for an input mask.

To block data from a field, first figure out exactly what data you want to allow in a field; then use the characters in the following table to code the data in the Input Mask field property in the table Design view.

| Input Mask Character | What It Allows/Requires |
| --- | --- |
| 0 | Requires a number; + and – not allowed |
| 9 | Allows a number; + and – not allowed |
| # | Allows a space, converts a blank to a space, allows + and – |
| L | Requires a letter |
| ? | Allows a letter |
| A | Requires a letter or number |
| a | Allows a letter or number |
| C | Allows any character or a space |
| < | Converts the following characters to lowercase |
| > | Converts the following characters to uppercase |
| ! | Fills field from right to left, allowing characters on the left side to be optional |
| \ | Displays the character following in the field (\Z appears as Z) |
| . , | Displays the decimal placeholder or thousands separator |
| ; : - / | Displays the date separator (the symbol used depends on the setting in the Regional Settings section of the Windows Control Panel) |

The Input Mask Wizard can help you enter the input mask for your data — especially if the data in the field is a common type of data, such as a phone number or a zip code.

To use the Input Mask Wizard, follow these steps:

*1.* Display the table in Design view.

*2.* Select the field to which you want to add an input mask.

*3.* Click Input Mask in the Field Properties pane of the window.

*4.* Click the Build button that appears to the right of the property.

Access displays the Input Mask Wizard (it may take a while). If you didn't install the Advanced Wizards when you installed Access 97, you get a message telling you that you must install them before proceeding. Find out how to install Advanced Wizards later in this section.

**5.** Select the input mask that looks like the data that you want to allow in the field.

**6.** Click the Try It box.

Access displays the field as it will look before data is entered — blanks are shown as underscores, and punctuation, like hyphens or parentheses, are displayed.

**7.** Type some text to see how the field will appear with data in it.

**8.** Click Next to see more questions about the Input Mask you've chosen. The questions you see depend on the type of data you chose in the first window. Access displays a Try It box on the window so that you can see the effect of any changes you make.

**Input Mask Wizard**

Which input mask matches how you want data to look?

To see how a selected mask works, use the Try It box.
To change the Input Mask list, click the Edit List button.

| Input Mask: | Data Look: |
|---|---|
| Zip Code | 98052-6399 |
| Social Security Number | 531-86-7180 |
| Phone Number | (206) 555-1212 |
| Extension | 63215 |
| Password | ******* |
| Short Time | 18:07 |

Try It:

Edit List    Cancel    < Back    Next >    Finish

Click Finish to accept the default settings and skip additional wizard windows.

**9.** If necessary, click Next to display the final window of the wizard.

**10.** Click Finish to tell the wizard to put the input mask it has helped you create into the Input Mask property for the field.

Access displays the Design view with the new Input Mask.

**11.** Save the table design by clicking the Save button — otherwise, you may lose your nifty new Input Mask!

You can't use the Input Mask Wizard unless the Advanced Wizards are installed on your computer — which won't be the case if you opted for the standard Access installation. If the Advanced Wizards are not installed, a message to that effect appears when you click the Build button to use the Input Mask Wizard.

To install the Advanced Wizards, you have to run Microsoft Office Setup again:

*1.* Close Access and run Microsoft Office Setup.

Use Windows Explorer or My Computer to find the Microsoft Office Setup shortcut. If you have a standard installation of Office 97, the shortcut is in C:\Program Files\Microsoft Office\. Double-click the Microsoft Office Setup item to run the Setup.

*2.* In the first screen, choose Add/Remove.

The next screen displays components of Microsoft Office.

*3.* Choose Access and click Change Option.

Up springs a window that enables you to tell the set-up program which pieces of Access you want to add or remove.

*4.* Click Advanced Wizards to place a check mark in the check box.

*5.* Click OK to close the Microsoft Office 97 – Microsoft Access dialog box.

*6.* Click Continue in the Microsoft Office 97 – Maintenance dialog box to tell the set-up program to install the Developer Tools.

*7.* When the Setup finishes installing the Advanced Wizards, it displays a dialog box telling you that Setup was completed successfully. Click OK and run Access. You can now use the Input Mask Wizard.

# Changing Column Width

Initially, Access gives all columns in a datasheet the same width. You can change the width one column at a time, or a few columns at once.

To change the width of one column, follow these steps:

*1.* Move the mouse pointer to the right border of the column and then up to the top of the column, where the field names appear.

The pointer turns into the change-column-width pointer.

*2.* Click and drag the column border to a new position.

You can change the width of several consecutive columns at the same time using the preceding method — simply select all the columns and then change the width of one of them. All the selected columns will have the same width as the one column whose width you changed.

You can also tell Access to change the column width so that the column is wide enough for the widest data in the column. To size the column to fit the contents, move the mouse pointer so that you see the "change column width" pointer, and double-click.

# Changing Data Types

Fields have to have a *type*, which describes the kind of data that can be entered into the field. Common data types are text, numeric, and date/time. The following table describes each data type:

| Data Type | What It Holds |
| --- | --- |
| Text | The Text type can contain numbers, letters, punctuation, spaces, and special characters (such as #, @, !, %). If you use hyphens or parentheses in phone numbers (and almost everyone does), the phone-number field is defined as a text field. If you put a number in a text field, you won't be able to use it in calculations (but who wants to add phone numbers?). A text field holds up to 255 characters. |
| Memo | The Memo type can contain Numbers, letters, spaces, and special characters, just like the Text type, but more of them fit in a Memo field than in a Text field — up to 65,535 characters. (You really have to work to fill this field up!) |
| Number | The Number type can only contain numbers — not even spaces are allowed. When you put your numbers in a Number field, you can use them later for calculations. |
| Date/Time | The Date/Time type can hold, well, dates and times. |
| Currency | The Currency type holds numbers with a currency sign in front of them ($, £, ¥, and so on). |
| AutoNumber | The AutoNumber type includes numbers unique to each record. Access assigns these numbers starting at 1, for the first record, and working up. |
| Yes/No | The Yes/No type holds any kind of yes-or-no data. You can set up a Yes/No field to contain other two-word sets, such as True/False, On/Off, and Male/Female, and so on. |
| OLE Object | The OLE Object type can hold a picture, a sound, or some other object that was created with software other than Access. |
| Hyperlink | The Hyperlink type contains World Wide Web addresses (URLs) or other kinds of hyperlink addresses. |
| Lookup Wizard | The Lookup Wizard type runs the Lookup Wizard, which enables you to tell Access to enter data in this field according to other criteria. If you have a list of people who are coming to a potluck dinner, and if people whose last names start with *A* through *F* are bringing a main course, you could define a lookup field to look at the last-name field and enter the food that each person is bringing. |

If you create your table in Datasheet view and enter data, Access guesses from the data that you entered what the data type is. If you entered text, Access makes the data type of the field Text. If you entered numbers with a currency symbol in front, Access sets the data type to Currency.

If you want to change the data type Access has chosen, you can do it by using the Data Type setting for the field in Design view. Follow these steps:

*1.* Switch to Design view by clicking the Design View button.

*2.* Find the name of the field for which you want to change the data type and click the Data Type column for that field name.

*3.* Display the drop-down list by clicking the down-arrow key or by pressing Alt+↓.

*4.* Choose the data type that you want by clicking it.

You can also cycle through the data types by double-clicking the Data Type setting.

## Changing Row Height

You can change row heights in the same way that you change column widths. Changing row height has a catch, though — when you change the height of one row, the heights of all the other rows in the datasheet change, too. If you make a row tall enough, Access wraps any text so that you can see more than one line of text in a field.

| Order ID | Item Descript | Item Number | Number of item | Cost per item | Shi |
|---|---|---|---|---|---|
| 1 | Rocking Bench | 7684 | 1 | $219.00 | |
| 1 | Cushion | 7623 | 1 | $54.95 | |
| 2 | Sleep T | 3162-0220 | 2 | $18.00 | |
| 3 | Newspaper Basket | 06-684-852 | 1 | $39.00 | |
| 3 | Divided rattan hamper | 06-680587 | 1 | $69.00 | |
| 3 | Basic bookcase | 06-770222 | 1 | $69.00 | |

Items ordered : Table
Record: 14 ◄ 1 ► ►I ►* of 7

Change the height of rows in a datasheet by following these steps:

*1.* Move the mouse pointer to the row selector (the gray box to the left of the first field).

*2.* Move the mouse pointer to the line between two rows.

The pointer turns into the change-row-height pointer.

*3.* Drag the row border up or down to make the row taller or shorter.

**TIP**

If you want to make a row exactly two lines tall, use the row borders as a guide as you drag the change-row-height pointer.

To change row height back to its standard height, follow these steps:

**1.** Right-click a row selector and choose <u>R</u>ow Height from the shortcut menu.

Access displays the Row Height dialog box.

| Row Height | ? X |
|---|---|
| <u>R</u>ow Height: `12.75` | OK |
| ☑ <u>S</u>tandard Height | Cancel |

**2.** Click the <u>S</u>tandard Height check box so that a check mark appears in it.

**3.** Click OK.

Access changes the row height back to the standard height.

## Copying a Field

You can copy a field. This capability is particularly useful if you are creating several similar fields — rather than define the data type and properties for each field, you can simply copy a field definition and edit the field as necessary.

Here's how to copy a field:

**1.** Display the table in Design view.

**2.** Select the field that you want to copy by clicking the row selector.

 **3.** Copy the field by clicking the Copy button or choosing <u>E</u>dit⇨<u>C</u>opy.

**4.** Move to a blank row or create a blank row.

 **5.** Click the Paste button or choose <u>E</u>dit⇨<u>P</u>aste.

Notice that Access copies the field properties as well as the information in the selected row.

**6.** Rename the copied field by typing a new name.

Access has the field name selected, so typing a new name replaces the selected name.

**7.** Press Enter to complete the new field.

**8.** Edit the Description, if necessary.

*9.* Save the table.

You can copy the field again by moving to another blank row and clicking the Paste button.

# Creating a Lookup Field

You can create your own drop-down list in a table to guide others (or yourself) as they enter data. A lookup field provides the user with a list of choices, rather than requiring users to type a value into the datasheet. Lookup fields enable you to keep your database small and the data entered in it accurate.

The items on this list may come from a list that you type or from entries in another table. For example, if you have an Employee table in your database to keep track of employee information, and a Checks table in the same database to keep track of each week's paychecks, you can ensure that the employees' names aren't misspelled in the Checks table by making the Name field in the Checks table a lookup field and linking it to the Employee table. Now you can tell Access to display a drop-down list in the Name field of the Checks table, which lists the names in the Name field in the Employee table. (It's not as confusing as it sounds. Trust me.)

Access has a Lookup Wizard to help you create lookup fields. Here's how to use it:

*1.* In Design view, display the table in which you want to put the lookup field.

*2.* Display the drop-down Data Type list of the field for which you're creating the list of possibilities.

*3.* Choose Lookup Wizard to display the first window of the Lookup Wizard.

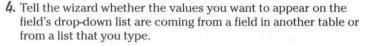

**4.** Tell the wizard whether the values you want to appear on the field's drop-down list are coming from a field in another table or from a list that you type.

If the field simply consists of several choices, choose the second option and type the list. But if you want to store more information about those choices (maybe you're entering a name of a customer who bought something, but you also want to store the customer's address and phone number in another table), store the values in a table.

If you don't want the drop-down list to display every value in the field in another table, you can base the drop-down list on a field in a query.

**5.** Click Next to display the next window of the Lookup Wizard.

What you see in the second window depends on which option you chose in the first window.

If you asked the lookup field to display values from another table, Access asks you about the name of the table.

If you told Access that you wanted to type in the values, you get a table in which you can type the lookup list.

**6.** If you're typing values to choose among, click in the table in the wizard window (which currently has only one cell), and type the first entry in the list. Press Tab — not Enter — to create new cells for additional entries.

If you want your lookup list to include values that are stored in another table, select the table that has the field with the values you want to choose among. You can choose an existing query by clicking the Queries or Both radio button.

**7.** Click Next to display the next window.

**8.** If you typed a list, the next screen you see is the last screen of the wizard — skip to Step 12. If you're using a table for the lookup, you have to tell Access which field(s) you want to use by moving field names from the Available Fields list box to the Selected Fields list box.

***See also*** "Working with Wizards," in Part I, for more information on choosing fields in windows such as this one.

**9.** Click Next to display the next window.

This window shows you a table with the values that will appear in the lookup list, and allows you to change the width of the column.

**10.** Change the width of the column if necessary.

You can change the width of the column to automatically fit the widest entry by double-clicking the right edge of the field name that appears at the top of the column.

***See also*** "Changing Column Width," earlier in this part.

**11.** Click Next to display the final window of this wizard.

**12.** Edit the name that Access has given the lookup column, if you want, and then click Finish to create the lookup column.

**13.** Now check out your lookup list by viewing your table in Datasheet view. When you click the field for which you created the lookup list, you see an arrow that indicates that a drop-down list is available. Click the arrow to see options in the list.

You can add values to an existing lookup list. If you typed values for the lookup list yourself, switch to Design view, click the field with the lookup, and click the Lookup tab in the Field Properties pane. You can add options to the Row Source — separate the values with a semicolon.

The lookup field is not automatically updated when you add additional items. Refresh the data in the lookup field by pressing F9.

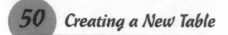 

# Creating a New Table

You create a table by using the New Table dialog box.

Display the New Table dialog box by doing any of the following things:

✦ Clicking New in the Tables tab of the Database window

✦ Choosing Insert⇨Table

✦ Clicking the New Object: Table button (If the New Object button shows an object other than a table, click the down arrow next to it and choose Table from the drop-down list.)

You have the following choices in the New Table dialog box:

| Choice | When to Use It |
|---|---|
| Datasheet View | To create a new table by entering data and field names in a spreadsheet-like table |
| Design View | To design the table in the table Design view by entering field names and data type, and perhaps using the more advanced Field Properties to define each field |
| Table Wizard | To use a wizard to choose from commonly used table formats |
| Import Table | To create a table by using a wizard to import data stored in another format |
| Link Table | To create a table by using a wizard to link your new table to an external data source |

***See also*** "Importing and Exporting Data," in Part VIII, for more information on using the Import and Link Table options.

## Creating a table in Datasheet view

Datasheet view is the most straightforward way to create a table. A datasheet looks like a spreadsheet — you can name your fields and begin entering data. Access figures out the type of data that each field holds.

Creating a table in Datasheet view does not prevent you from using the more advanced settings in Design view. To display Design view at any time, click the Design View button.

Generally, tables hold only raw data, such as numbers, text, and dates. Calculations are reserved for queries, reports, and forms. Including calculations in tables dramatically and unnecessarily increases the size of the database.

Here's how to create a table in Datasheet view:

**1.** Choose Insert⇨Table (or click New on the Tables tab of the Database window) to display the New Table dialog box.

**2.** Click OK (Datasheet View is already selected).

Access creates a table called Table1. Across the top of the table are field names: Field1, Field2, and so on.

**3.** (Optional) Enter one record of data (fill in the first row), and move to the next field by pressing Tab or Enter.

| ▦ Table1 : Table | | | | | | _ □ × |
|---|---|---|---|---|---|---|
| Field1 | Field2 | Field3 | Field4 | Field5 | Field6 | Field7 ▲ |
| ▶| | | | | | | |
| | | | | | | |
| | | | | | | |
| | | | | | | |
| | | | | | | |
| | | | | | | |
| | | | | | | |
| | | | | | | |
| | | | | | | |
| | | | | | | ▼ |
| Record: ⏮ ◀ | 1 ▶ ⏭ ▶* of 30 | ◀ | | | ▶ | |

Access displays a pencil icon in the left border of the row to indicate that you are entering or changing data.

**4.** Rename the fields by double-clicking the field name, typing a new name, and pressing Enter. Give the fields names that reflect the data contained in them.

***See also*** "Renaming a Field," later in this part.

**5.** Enter the rest of your data, if you want.

To move to the beginning of a row, press the Home key. To move to the next line, press the ↓ key.

***See also*** "Adding Data to Your Database," earlier in this part.

**6.** Save the table by clicking the Save button, pressing Ctrl+S, or choosing File⇨Save.

Access displays the Save As dialog box.

**7.** Type a new name for the table (it's helpful to give tables names that indicate what data is stored in them), and press Enter.

To accept the name that Access suggests, simply press Enter.

**8.** When Access asks whether you want to define a primary key, choose Yes or No. If you're not sure, choose No — you can go back to the table later to define a primary key, if you need to.

*See also* "Identifying Records with a Primary Key," later in this part.

**9.** Close the table by clicking its Close button.

## Creating a table in Design view

Design view is a good place to create your table if you want to use the more advanced settings, called *field properties,* that are available only in this view. Otherwise, Datasheet view usually works best.

*Remember:* You can only define fields in Design view — you can't enter any data. You have to use the Datasheet view or a form to do that.

To use Design view to create a table, follow these steps:

**1.** Choose Insert⇨Table (or click New on the tables tab of the Database window) to display the New Table dialog box.

**2.** Select Design View and click OK (or simply double-click Design View).

Access displays a Design view for the new, blank table. The cursor is in the first row, below the Field Name column heading.

**3.** Type the name of the first field; then press Enter or Tab to move to the Data Type column.

Access displays the default Data Type, which is Text. As soon as the you establish a data type for a field, Access displays field properties for that type of data in the Field Properties pane of the Design view window.

**4.** To view all data types, press Alt+↓ (or click the down arrow) to display the drop-down list of data type options.

**5.** Select the appropriate data type for the field.

*See also* "Changing Data Types," earlier in this part.

**6.** (Optional) Type a description in the third column, the one labeled Description.

The description that you type appears in the status bar whenever the field is selected. Typing a description can give you and other users a hint about using the field.

**7.** Define additional fields in the table by repeating Steps 3 through 5.

**8.** Define a primary key by putting the cursor in the row with the primary key field and clicking the Primary Key button on the toolbar. Access displays a key to the left of the field name.

*See also* "Identifying Records with a Primary Key," later in this part.

**9.** Click the Save button or press Ctrl+S to display the Save As dialog box.

**10.** Type a new name for the table and then press Enter.

To enter data after you design the table, click the Datasheet View button to display Datasheet view. *See also* "About Tables" and "Adding Data to Your Database" in this part.

## Creating a table using the Table Wizard

The Table Wizard simplifies the process of creating a table by allowing you to choose from among some common tables and often-used fields.

To create a table with the Table Wizard, follow these steps:

**1.** Choose Insert⇨Table (or click New on the Tables tab of the Database window) to display the New Table dialog box.

**2.** Select Table Wizard, and choose OK.

Access displays the first window of the Table Wizard.

**Table Wizard**

Which of the sample tables listed below do you want to use to create your table?

After selecting a sample table, choose the sample fields you want to include in your new table. Your table can include fields from more than one sample table. If you're not sure about a field, go ahead and include it. It's easy to delete a field later.

Sample Tables:

Mailing List
Contacts
Customers
Employees
Products
Orders
Order Details

○ Business
○ Personal

Sample Fields:

MailingListID
Prefix
FirstName
MiddleName
LastName
Suffix
Nickname
Title
OrganizationName
Address

Fields in my new table:

Rename Field...

Cancel | < Back | Next > | Finish

**3.** If your database is for personal rather than business use, click the Personal radio button in the bottom-left corner to display tables and sample fields that are commonly used in personal applications.

**4.** Select a table in the Sample Tables list.

The field names in the Sample Fields list change to reflect the table that you selected. (Don't forget to use the scroll bars to see all the options.)

**5.** Add fields to the Fields in my new table list by double-clicking the field name in the Sample Fields list. You can select all the fields in the Sample Fields list by clicking the double-right-arrow button.

The selected field(s) appears in the Fields in My New Table list.

**6.** If necessary, remove fields from the Fields in My New Table list.

To remove one field name, select it and then click the left-arrow button to the left of the Fields in My New Table list. To remove all fields (maybe you need to start over!), click the double left-facing arrow.

**7.** (Optional) You can rename a field by selecting it in the Fields in My New Table list and clicking the Rename Field button.

Access displays the Rename Field dialog box. Type the new name or edit the name displayed in the dialog box, and press Enter.

At any time after you select the table and fields, you can click
Finish to accept the Table Wizard defaults and create the table.

**8.** Click Next to display the next Table Wizard window.

**9.** Change the name of the table (if you think it needs a better
name) and use the radio buttons to tell Access whether you want
it to set a primary key.

**10.** Click Next to display the next window. This window asks if any
fields in the new table are related to any existing tables in the
database.

**11.** If fields in the new table are related to fields in an existing table,
select the table and click the Relationships button. Use the
Relationships dialog box to tell Access how the tables are
related; then click OK.

**12.** Click Next to display the last window.

**13.** Click the radio button that describes what you want to do when
the table is created.

**14.** Click Finish to create the table.

*See also* "Working with Wizards," in Part I.

# Customizing Fields Using the Field Properties Pane

*Field properties,* which appear at the bottom of a window in Design
view, enable you to format a field and disallow certain entries. The
part of the Design view that contains the field properties is called the
*Field Properties pane* (a pane being part of a window — cute, eh?).
The properties that you see in this pane depend on the data type that
you choose. Although many properties appear for all data types, not
all properties appear for all data types.

To change a field property, you have to tell Access which field you're
working with. Display your table in Design view and click somewhere in the row that contains the field you want to work with. You
can also click the row selector — the gray box to the left of the field
name. (The field you're currently working with has an arrow in the
row selector.)

Selected row/field

Row selector

Field properties

| Field Name | Data Type | Description |
|---|---|---|
| Item ID | AutoNumber | |
| Item Description | Memo | |
| Item Number | Text | |
| Number of items | Number | |
| Cost per item | Currency | |
| Total Cost for Item | Currency | |
| Shipping | Currency | |
| Memo | Memo | |
| Order ID | Number | |

**Field Properties**

General | Lookup

| | |
|---|---|
| Field Size | Integer |
| Format | General Number |
| Decimal Places | Auto |
| Input Mask | |
| Caption | |
| Default Value | 0 |
| Validation Rule | |
| Validation Text | |
| Required | No |
| Indexed | Yes (Duplicates OK) |

The data type determines the kind of values that users can store in the field. Press F1 for help on data types.

The field properties shown in the preceding figure are for a Number type field. The properties you see vary depending on the type of field that's active.

Access can help you format field properties. Click a property; if you see an arrow to the right of the property, Access has predefined settings for that property. If you see a Build button to the right of the property, click that button to display a dialog box or wizard that helps fill in the property for you.

***See also*** "Blocking Unwanted Data with an Input Mask," "Limiting Data Entries with a Validation Rule," "Formatting Fields," and "Setting Field Size," all in this part, for information about using Field Properties.

# Deleting a Field

You can delete a field from a table, but you should do so very carefully — a 24-hour waiting period may be in order. When you delete a field (which is a column in a datasheet), you also irretrievably delete all the data in the field.

To delete a field in Datasheet view, follow these steps:

*1.* Right-click the field name for the column.

Access selects the column and displays the shortcut menu.

*2.* Choose Delete Column from the shortcut menu.

Access displays a warning box, telling you that you will be permanently deleting the field and the data in it.

**3.** Click Yes to delete the field (or No if you change your mind).

To delete a field in Design view, follow the same procedure, except right-click the row selector for the field that you want to delete and choose Delete Rows from the shortcut menu.

# Deleting Records

To delete a record in a datasheet, follow these steps:

**1.** Right-click the row selector of the record that you want to delete.

**2.** Choose Delete Record from the shortcut menu.

 Alternatively, you can put the cursor anywhere in the row that you want to delete and then click the Delete Record button.

Deleting a record is permanent. When you delete data, you can't get it back — so make sure that you really want to delete it!

# Editing Data in a Datasheet

Edit a value by moving the cursor to the value, pressing F2, or clicking on the value to see a cursor. Delete characters by using the Delete and Backspace keys. Add new characters by typing them.

To replace the contents of a field, select the entire field by clicking at the beginning of the field, holding the mouse button down, and sliding the mouse pointer to the end of the field. Go ahead and type the new entry — anything that you type replaces the selected characters.

*See also* "Moving Around in a Datasheet," later in this part.

# Filtering Your Data

Filtering allows you to look at a subset of your table — records that match a particular criteria. (In English, this means that you can create a test for your data to pass, and then only look at the lines in your table that pass your test.) In Access, a criterion for filtering is something like "I want to find all the records with 2 in the Number of Items field." To use more advanced criteria such as "2 or more" or "between 3 and 20," you need to use the Advanced Filter/Sort command. *See also* "Sorting a Query," in Part IV.

When filtering doesn't give you the options you need, you probably need to use a query. *See also* "Creating Action Queries," in Part IV.

You can filter in three ways: Filter by Selection, Filter by Form, and Advanced Filter/Sort. The following table explains when you need to use each filtering option:

| Type of Filter | When You Need to Use It |
| --- | --- |
| Filter by Selection | When you have only one criterion that filtered records need to meet, and you can find one record that matches your criterion. |
| Filter by Form | When you have more than one criterion to match. |
| Advanced Filter/Sort | When what you really want to do is create a query, using one table. (Choosing Advanced Filter/Sort creates a query.) |

Filtering creates a temporary table that contains only the records that fit the criteria. If you want a permanent table that updates as more records are added, you need to create a query.

## Filter by Selection

To filter by selection, you first need to find a record that matches your criterion. If you want to find all the Virginia addresses in your address table, for example, you need to find an address that has VA in the State field.

Follow these steps to filter a table by selection:

*1.* Put the cursor in the record and field that matches the criterion.

To find all addresses in Virginia, for example, you may put the cursor in the State field that contains the abbreviation VA.

*2.* Click the Filter by Selection button or choose Records➪Filter➪Filter by Selection.

Access creates a temporary table that consists of the records that meet the criterion.

If you haven't narrowed the list down enough, you can filter the filtered table again by using the same technique. You can choose a different field, or even select just one word or part of a field, before clicking the Filter by Selection button.

To see the entire table again, click the Apply Filter button.

You can select particular records that you want to filter out and then choose Records➪Filter➪Filter Excluding Selection to exclude the selected records from the table. Use this technique in combination with the Filter by Selection command to see only the records you want to see. To see the entire table, click the Apply Filter button again.

## Filter by Form

If you have more than one criterion, you should filter by form. The Filter by Form window enables you to pick values that you want filtered records to have. Unlike the Filter by Selection command, however, Filter by Form allows you to choose more than one value and to choose values to match for more than one field.

When you Filter by Form, you can use multiple criteria. If you specify more than one criterion on a Filter by Form tab, Access treats the criteria as AND criteria, meaning that a record has to pass *all* the criteria in order to be displayed on the filtered datasheet.

If you use criteria on different tabs (using the OR tab at the bottom of the window to display a clean grid), Access treats the criteria as OR criteria. That means that a record only has to pass the criteria on one tab or the other to be displayed on the filtered datasheet.

Using AND and OR criteria enables you to filter the records using more than one rule or set of rules. For example, you can find addresses from San Francisco, CA, as well as addresses in Massachusetts by using the OR tab at the bottom of the Filter by Form window.

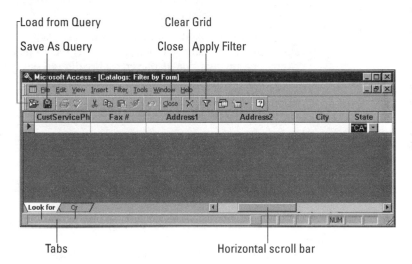

Follow these steps to filter a datasheet by form:

**1.** Click the Filter by Form button or choose Records➪Filter➪Filter by Form.

Access displays the Filter by Form window, which looks like an empty datasheet with some different buttons in the toolbar, and some different menu choices.

**2.** The field that the cursor was in contains a value and a down arrow; if that's not a field that you want to use in your filter criteria, press Delete to delete the critieria and then click a field that you have a criterion for.

A down arrow appears in the field that the cursor is in.

**3.** Click the arrow to see the list of all the values for that field.

**4.** Click the value that you want the filtered records to match.

If you want the criteria to specify part of the value in the field, type **LIKE** *"value that you're looking for."* For example, LIKE "n" in the Name field finds all records in the Name field that have the letter *n* in them.

**5.** If you have criteria for another field that should be applied at the same time as the criterion you set in Step 4 (AND criteria), repeat Steps 3 and 4 for the additional field.

For example, if you want to find addresses in San Francisco, CA, set the State field to CA, and the City field to San Francisco.

**6.** If you have another set of rules to filter records by, click the Or tab at the bottom of the Filter by Form window.

Access displays a blank Filter by Form window. When you set criteria on more than one tab, a record only has to meet the criteria on one tab to be displayed on the filtered datasheet.

**7.** Choose the criteria on the second tab in the same way that you chose those on the first — click the field, and choose the value that you want to match.

For example, if you also want to see all addresses from Boston, MA, set the State field on the new Filter by Form grid to MA, and the City field to Boston.

Another Or tab appears, allowing you to continue adding as many sets of OR criteria as you need.

**8.** To see the filtered table, click the Apply Filter button.

You have a few more options when you use the Filter by Form window:

| If You Want to . . . | Here's How to Do It |
| --- | --- |
| Delete a tab's worth of criteria | Click the tab and then choose Edit➪Delete Tab. |
| Delete all criteria | Click the Clear Grid button. |

| *If You Want to . . .* | *Here's How to Do It* |
|---|---|
| Save the filter as a query, so that you can see it later | Click the Save As Query button, give the new query a name, and click the OK button. To see the query, click the Queries tab of the Database window. |
| See the entire table | Click the Apply Filter button. |
| See the filtered table again | Click the Apply Filter button. |
| Use an expression as a criterion | Type the expression in the field to which it applies. *See also* "Limiting Records with Criteria Expressions," in Part IV. |

## Finding Data in a Table

When you need to find a record that contains a particular word or value, use the Find dialog box.

To display the Find dialog box, display a datasheet and do one of the following:

✦ Press Ctrl+F.

✦ Choose Edit➪Find.

✦ Click the Find button.

To use the Find dialog box, follow these steps:

**1.** In Datasheet view, put the cursor in the field that contains the value that you are searching for.

**2.** Display the Find dialog box.

**3.** In the Find What box, type the text or value that you're looking for.

**4.** Click Find First to find the first instance of the value or text in the table.

Access displays the part of the table where it found the contents of the Find What box.

**5.** If you have not found what you're looking for, click Find Next until you do.

Use the settings in the Find dialog box to find exactly what you're looking for:

+ **Search:** This option determines the direction in which Access searches. Choose Up, Down, or All. Choose All to find the text or value anywhere in the table. Regardless of what you choose, when you click Find First, Access finds the first instance of the text or value in the entire table. If you want to search up or down from the current record, make sure to click Find Next.

+ **Match:** Choose Any Part of Field, Whole Field, or Start of Field to tell Access whether the value or text that you typed is in the entire field, at the beginning of the field, or anywhere in the field (which means that the text may start somewhere in the middle of the field).

+ **Match Case:** When you check this check box, Access finds only text that matches the case of the text that you typed in the Find What box.

+ **Search Fields As Formatted:** This option matches the contents of the Find What box to the formatted data (the way the data appears in the table, using the Format and Input Mask properties, rather than the way it was entered). *See also* "Customizing Fields Using the Field Properties Pane," earlier in this part.

+ **Search Only Current Field:** This option searches only the field that the cursor was in when you displayed the Find dialog box. If you want to search the whole datasheet, make sure that this option is turned off.

When you know which field you want to search, use the Search Only Current field check box to make the search quicker.

# Formatting Datasheets

Although you don't have the flexibility in formatting datasheets that you do with reports and forms, you do have some options. You can change the font, row height, column width, and some other options. To change a datasheet's format, use the Format menu. (A datasheet has to be the active window for you to see this menu.)

## Changing the font

You can change the font and font size in your datasheet by using the Font dialog box. Display the datasheet, then follow these steps:

*1.* Choose Format⇨Font.

Access displays the Font dialog box.

Sample box

**2.** Choose a different font from the Font list.

Notice that the sample text changes to display the font that you choose.

**3.** If you want to, change the font Size, Font Style, and even the font Color.

**4.** Click OK to see the datasheet with its new font settings.

## Displaying and removing gridlines

*Gridlines* are the gray horizontal and vertical lines that separate cells in a datasheet. You can change the color of the gridlines displayed in a datasheet or not display gridlines at all. You can also give cells some special effects, rather than simply separate them with gridlines.

To change gridlines, choose Format➪Cells. Access displays the Cell Effect dialog box.

As you change the settings, the Sample box shows the effect that the changes have on the datasheet.

Here's what the options on the Cell Effect dialog box do to your datasheet:

| Setting | What It Does |
|---|---|
| Horizontal | Displays or hides horizontal gridlines |
| Vertical | Displays or hides vertical gridlines |
| Cell Effect: Flat, Raised, or Sunken | Displays the cells normally (Flat) or with a three-dimensional effect |
| Gridline Color | Allows you to choose a gridline color |
| Background Color | Allows you to choose a background color for cells |

# Formatting Fields

When you're working with a table in Design view, you can format various fields by using the Format setting in the Field Properties pane.

## Formatting Text and Memo fields

When you're dealing with a Text field, the Format options of the Field Properties pane enable you to specify how the text in a field should appear, as well as how many characters a person may enter in the field.

To format Text and Memo fields, type the characters in the following table into the Format section of the Field Properties pane.

| Formatting for Text | What You Type |
|---|---|
| Display text all uppercase | > |
| Display text all lowercase | < |
| Display text left-aligned | ! |
| Specify a color | [*color*] (black, blue, green, cyan, magenta, yellow, and white are allowed colors) |
| Specify a certain number of characters | @ (Type @ for each character to be included — even spaces) |
| Specify that no character is required | & |
| Display text | /text |

You can tell Access to add characters such as +, –, $, (, and ) or a space to the data that is entered. For example, you may want to enter the following in the Format setting for a phone number:

( @@@ )@@@-@@@@

If someone then enters ten digits into this field, the numbers would appear with parentheses and the hyphen, even though the user didn't type the extra characters.

You can even format fields to include additional text. Just enclose the text you want to add in quotation marks or precede it with a slash (/).

You can use the Input Mask option to help you with formatting. *See also* "Blocking Unwanted Data with an Input Mask," earlier in this part.

## Formatting Number and Currency fields

Access has common formats for Number and Currency fields built right in — all you have to do is choose the format that you want from the Format drop-down list in the Field Properties pane.

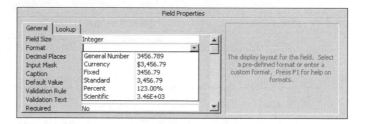

The following tables describe the different formats from which you can choose:

| Number Format | How It Works |
| --- | --- |
| Number | Displays numbers without commas and with as many decimal places as the user enters |
| Currency | Displays numbers with the local currency symbol (determined from the Regional in the Windows 95 Control Panel), commas as thousands separators, and two decimal places |
| Fixed | Displays numbers with the number of decimal places specified in the Decimal Places setting (immediately below the Format setting); the default is 2 |
| Standard | Displays numbers with commas as thousands separators and the number of decimal places specified in the Decimal Places property |
| Percent | Displays numbers as percentages — that is, multiplied by 100 and followed by a percent sign |
| Scientific | Displays numbers in scientific notation |

If the numbers in the field don't seem to be formatted according to the Number Format property, you may need to change the Field Size property. For example, if you have the Field Size property set to Integer or Long Integer, it doesn't matter what value you use in the Decimal Places property, Access will insist on displaying the value as an integer — with no decimal places. Try Single or Double in the Format property, instead.

You can define your own number format by using the following symbols in the Format field property instead of choosing from the drop-down list:

| Symbol | What It Does |
|---|---|
| # | Displays a value if one is input for that place |
| 0 | Displays a 0 if no value appears in that place; otherwise, displays the input value |
| . | Displays a decimal point |
| , | Displays a comma |
| $ (or other currency symbol) | Displays a currency symbol |
| % | Displays the number in percent format |
| E+00 | Displays scientific notation |

You can, for example, create a number format with comma separators and three decimal places by typing the following in the Format property:

*###,##0.000*

## Formatting Date/Time fields

Access has built-in Date/Time formats from which you can choose. To see these formats, display the drop-down list in the Format section of the Field Properties pane.

Next to each format name is an example of how the date and/or time is displayed. If you don't specify a format for a Date/Time field, Access uses the General Date format.

| General Date | 6/19/94 5:34:23 PM |
|---|---|
| Long Date | Sunday, June 19, 1994 |
| Medium Date | 19-Jun-94 |
| Short Date | 6/19/94 |
| Long Time | 5:34:23 PM |
| Medium Time | 5:34 PM |
| Short Time | 17:34 |

You can create your own Date/Time format if you don't like the ones that Access offers on the drop-down list. To see what characters you can use to create your own Date/Time format, do the following:

*1.* Make sure that the selected field is a Date/Time field.

*2.* Move your cursor to the Format field property.

*3.* Press F1.

Access displays general help on the Format property.

To see help specific to creating your own Date/Time format, click the Date/Time Data Type link, about 13 lines down from the top of the Help window.

# Freezing a Column in a Datasheet

When you're working with a wide datasheet, you may want to freeze one column so that you can move all the way to the right edge of the table and still see a particular field. When you freeze a column, it moves to the left side of the window (no matter where it appeared before) and stays there when you scroll or pan all the way to the right.

To freeze a column, follow these steps:

*1.* Right-click the field name to select the column and display the shortcut menu.

*2.* Select Free*z*e Columns to freeze the selected column.

You can select more than one consecutive column to freeze by clicking the first field name and dragging to the last one, but then you have to choose *F*ormat⇨Freeze Columns from the menu to freeze the columns. You can't display the shortcut menu without deselecting all but one of the columns.

To unfreeze a column, choose *F*ormat⇨Unfreeze *A*ll Columns.

# Hiding a Column in a Datasheet

A hidden column is still in your datasheet; you just can't see it. Here's how to hide a column:

*1.* Right-click the field name to select the column and display the shortcut menu.

*2.* Choose *H*ide Columns from the shortcut menu.

Access hides the selected column.

You can select more than one consecutive column to hide by clicking the first field name and dragging to the last one, but then you have to choose Format⇨Hide Columns from the menu to hide the columns. You can't display the shortcut menu without deselecting all but one of the columns.

To make hidden columns reappear, try this:

*1.* Choose Format⇨Unhide Columns.

Access displays the Unhide Columns dialog box.

*2.* Click a check box to change the setting for the column.

Field names with check marks are displayed; field names without check marks are hidden.

*3.* Choose OK to close the dialog box and redisplay the datasheet. Fields are hidden or displayed depending on the settings on the Unhide Columns dialog box.

# Identifying Records with a Primary Key

A *primary key* uniquely identifies every record in the table. Most of the time, the primary key is a single field, but it can also be a combination of fields, in which case it is called a *multiple-field primary key.*

You can identify an existing field as the primary key, or you can ask Access to create one. To have Access create a primary key for you, follow these steps:

*1.* Close the table.

Access asks whether you want to create a primary key.

*2.* Select Yes.

Access creates a field called ID in the first column of the table. The field starts at 1 and increases by 1 for each record (it's an AutoNumber field). Access automatically inserts a new number each time you add a new record to the table.

You can also create a primary key in Design view. Click the cursor in the field that is the primary key and click the Primary Key button. Access displays the key symbol to the left of the field name.

To make a *multiple-field primary key,* select the fields in Design view. To select a field, click the row selector — the gray block to the left of the field name. Then Ctrl+click to select fields after you select the first field. When the fields are selected, click the Primary Key button.

# Indexing a Field

An index speeds querying, sorting, and grouping. If you plan to look for a specific value in a specific field over and over, you can save yourself some time by setting up an index for that field.

*Note:* Key fields are indexed automatically.

To tell Access to index a field, follow these steps:

*1.* Display the table in Design view.

*2.* Select the field for which you want to create an index.

*3.* Display the Indexed drop-down list under the General tab of the Field Properties pane.

*4.* Choose one of the two Yes options.

The Indexed field property offers three choices:

✦ **No:** The field is not indexed.

✦ **Yes (Duplicates OK):** The field is indexed.

✦ **Yes (No Duplicates):** The field is indexed, and Access won't allow two records in this field to have the same value. Key fields always have this setting (by definition, a value in a key field must be unique), and you can use this setting in other fields in which repetitions are undesirable.

# Inserting a Column or Adding a Field

Inserting a column into a datasheet gives you the space to add a new field to the table. You can also add a field to your table using Design view.

To add a field in Design view, follow these steps:

*1.* Right-click the row selector of the field that will be immediately after the field that you are going to insert.

Access selects the row and displays the shortcut menu.

*2.* Choose Insert Rows from the shortcut menu.

Access adds a row. Now you can define your field.

To add a column in Datasheet view, follow these steps:

*1.* Right-click the field name of the column that will be to the right of the new column.

Access selects the column and displays the shortcut menu.

**2.** Choose Insert Column from the shortcut menu.

# Limiting Data Entries with a Validation Rule

Often, you know exactly what kind of data you want people to type in a certain field. The Validation Rule field property (in the Field Properties pane) enables you to specify the kind of data that people can enter in a particular field.

If someone using your database attempts to enter data that does not pass your validation rule, the contents of the Validation Text field property pops up to guide the user.

Access has some rules about the two field properties that it uses to validate data:

✦ The *validation rule* cannot be longer than 2,048 characters.

✦ The *validation text* cannot be longer than 255 characters.

✦ String values in the validation rule must be enclosed in quotation marks.

✦ Data values in the validation rule must be enclosed in pound signs (#).

Use *operators* to tell Access how to validate your data. *Operators* are symbols like < and > and words like AND and NOT that you use to tell Access how to limit your data. (+, –, *, and / are also operators, but you aren't as likely to use them in validation rules.)

| Validation Rule Example | How It Works |
|---|---|
| "Boston" OR "New York" | Limits input in the field to just those two cities. |
| Is Null | The user is allowed to leave the field blank. |
| <10 | Only values less than 10 are allowed. |
| >10 | Only values greater than 10 are allowed. |
| <=10 | Only values less than or equal to 10 are allowed. |
| >=10 | Only values greater than or equal to 10 are allowed. |
| =10 | Only values equal to 10 are allowed. |
| <>0 | Only values not equal to 0 are allowed. |
| IN("Boston", "Concord") | Only text that is *Boston* or *Concord* is allowed. |
| BETWEEN 10 AND 20 | Only values between 10 and 20 are allowed. |

The LIKE operator deserves its own explanation. Use the LIKE operator to test whether an input matches a certain pattern — use wildcard characters to help define the pattern.

| Wildcard | What It Signifies |
| --- | --- |
| ? | Any single character |
| # | Any single number |
| * | Zero or more characters |

For example, you may define a zip code field to only allow five digits, as follows:

```
LIKE "#####"
```

You could also define a field to contain only names that start with the letter S, as follows:

```
LIKE "S*"
```

According to the preceding rule, a person can choose not to type any characters after the S because the * allows zero or more characters. If you want the S to always be followed by a certain number of characters, use the ? wildcard instead. For example, if you want people to type exactly three characters after the letter S, use this validation rule:

```
LIKE "S???"
```

You can use more than one expression in a validation rule by separating the expressions with AND, OR, or NOT. AND and NOT limit the entries that pass the rule. In the case of AND, an entry must pass both rules; in the case of NOT, and entry must pass one rule and fail the other. Using OR increases the likelihood that an entry will pass the rule because the entry only needs to pass one of the two rules separated by OR.

To create a validation rule, follow these steps:

**1.** Display the table in Design view.

**2.** Select the field to which you want to add a validation rule.

**3.** Click Validation Rule in the General tab of the Field Properties pane.

**4.** Click the Build button that appears to the right of the property.

The Expression Builder appears, ready to help you build your validation rule. *See also* "Calculating Fields (Building Expressions)" in Part IV, for more about using the Expression Builder.

# Moving a Column in a Datasheet

Move a column heading (the entire column goes with it) in Datasheet view by dragging it. Follow these steps:

**1.** Click the field that you want to move.

Access selects the column.

**2.** Click the field name a second time and drag to the column to its new position.

The mouse pointer turns into the move pointer (as I call it), and a dark line appears where the column is going.

**3.** When the dark line is in the position you want the column in, release the mouse button.

# Moving Around in a Datasheet

You can move around a datasheet in three ways: with the mouse, with keystrokes, and with the VCR buttons at the bottom of the datasheet window.

## Using the mouse

The most intuitive way to move around a datasheet is to use the mouse. To move to a specific place in the datasheet, simply click it.

You can also use the vertical and horizontal scroll bars to move around. Use these methods to move around a datasheet by using the scroll bars:

✦ Click either of the arrows at the end of the scroll bar to move one row or one column at a time.

✦ Click between the scroll box and an arrow at the end of the scroll bar to move one screen at a time.

✦ Click and drag the scroll box to a new position. When you are dragging the scroll box on the vertical scroll bar, a pop-up box will appear to tell you which record will be displayed when you release the mouse button.

The new IntelliMouse gives you another method, called *panning,* to move around a datasheet. To pan, hold down the wheel as you move the mouse pointer out of the datasheet window. The datasheet pans to show you the data out of view in the direction you moved the mouse. Be aware, though, that the cursor does not move. To move the cursor to a new position, click where you want it to be.

## Using the keyboard

If you get tired of taking your hands off the keyboard to use the mouse, start using keystrokes that move the cursor around the datasheet.

When you read the tables, it may help to think of fields as columns and records as rows.

You can use these keystrokes to move around a datasheet:

| Key to Press | Where It Takes You |
|---|---|
| PgUp | Up one screen |
| PgDn | Down one screen |
| Ctrl+PgUp | Left one screen |
| Ctrl+PgDn | Right one screen |
| Tab | Following field |
| Shift+Tab | Preceding field |
| Home | First field of the current record |
| End | Last field of the current record |
| ↑ | Up one record |
| ↓ | Down one record |
| Ctrl+↑ | First record of the current field |
| Ctrl+↓ | Last record of the current field |
| Ctrl+Home | First record of the first field (the top-left corner of the datasheet) |
| Ctrl+End | Last record of the last field (the bottom-right corner of the datasheet) |
| F5 | Specified record (type a record number and press Enter to go to a specific record) |

## Using the VCR buttons

Datasheet view has buttons at the bottom of the window that help you find the record that you need. You can click the buttons to move to the first or last record, to move up or down one record, or to move to a specific record number.

When you know the record number you want, type it in the record-number box and press Enter.

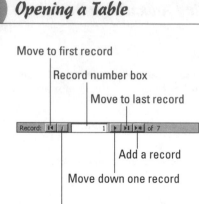

Move to first record

Record number box

Move to last record

Record: |◄| |/| | 1 |►| |►|| |►*| of 7

Add a record

Move down one record

Move up one record

# Naming Fields

The rules for naming Access fields are simple:

✦ Start with a letter or a number. (Actually, this is not a hard and fast rule, but it's good practice.)

✦ Don't use more than 64 characters.

In general, you want to keep your field names short, but long enough to tell you something about the data. (You can also use the Description in Design view to give the field a longer name.) If you ever want to use your database in a real SQL environment (for example, move it out of Access to another database application), don't use spaces in field names.

# Opening a Table

To open a table, follow these steps:

*1.* Display the Database window (the easiest way is to click the Database Window button).

*2.* Select the Tables tab.

*3.* Select the table that you want to open.

*4.* Click Open or double-click the table name to open the table in Datasheet view.

Click Design or Ctrl+double-click the name of the table to open it in Design view.

You can also open a table in Datasheet view by using a shortcut menu. Right-click a table name in the Database window, and choose Open from the shortcut menu.

# Renaming a Field

Changing the name of a field before you finish designing a table is a hassle-free task.

To rename a field, follow these steps:

*1.* Double-click the field name.

Access selects the entire name.

*2.* Type a new name for the field.

Alternatively, you can edit the current name by pressing F2 to deselect the name but remain in edit mode. Then press the Backspace and Delete keys to remove unnecessary characters, and type new characters.

*3.* Press Enter to enter the new name, or press Esc to cancel the renaming procedure.

If you change the name of a field after you complete the table and use the field name in queries, forms and reports, you have to change the name of the field each time it is used in another object. Unless you have a very compelling reason, don't rename fields after you use the field names in other objects — it's more trouble than it's worth.

# Saving a Table

To save a table (the design and the contents), follow these steps:

*1.* Make sure the table is active.

If the table is active, the color of its title bar matches the color of the Access title bar. You can click a window to make it active.

*2.* Click the Save button, press Ctrl+S, or choose File⇨Save.

You can also save a table by closing it. If you have made changes in a table since the last time you used it, when you close the table, Access asks whether you want to save it.

# Setting Field Size

For Text and Memo fields, use the Field Size option in the Field Properties pane of the table in Design view to limit input in the field to a specific number of characters. For Number data, the Field Size defines the type of number, and tells Access how much space is required to store each value.

The following are the Field Size options for numeric data:

| Numeric Field Size Settings | What They Do |
| --- | --- |
| Byte | Allows values from 0 to 255 with no decimal places |
| Integer | Allows values from –32,768 to 32,767 with no decimal places |
| Long Integer | Allows values from about negative 2 billion to about positive 2 billion with no decimal places |
| Double | Allows really huge numbers, both positive and negative, with up to 15 decimal places |
| Single | Allows not-quite-as-huge numbers, both positive and negative, with up to seven decimal places |

If you shorten the field size after entering data, you risk losing data when Access truncates entries longer than the new field size. The default field size for Text data, for example, is 50 characters. If you change the field-size setting to 25, all entries in the field that are longer than 25 characters will be truncated to 25 characters.

# Sorting Your Data

Your data may have been entered randomly, but it doesn't have to stay that way. Use the Sort commands (or buttons) to sort your data.

Before you sort, you have to know what you want to sort by. Do you want the Addresses table in order by last name, for example, or by zip code? When you know which field you want to sort by, sorting is a piece of cake.

You can sort in ascending order or descending order. *Ascending order* means that you start with the smallest number or the letter nearest the beginning of the alphabet, and work up from there. When you sort in ascending order, fields starting with *A* are at the top of the table, and fields starting with *Z* are at the bottom. *Descending order* is the opposite.

Follow these steps to sort a table in Datasheet view:

*1.* Select the field that you want to sort by (sometimes called the *sort key*) by clicking the field name.

If you don't select the column (and you don't have to), Access sorts by using the field that the cursor is in as the sort key.

**2.** Click the Sort Ascending or Sort Descending button, depending on which order you want to sort in.

If, for some strange reason, you prefer taking extra steps, you can use the menu. Choose Records⇨Sort⇨Sort Ascending or Records⇨Sort⇨Sort Descending.

# Splitting a Table with the Table Analyzer Wizard

The best way to split a table is to use the Table Analyzer Wizard to determine how to eliminate repeated information in a table. The Table Analyzer Wizard suggests fields to put in new tables to make the entire database more efficient.

Here's how to use the Table Analyzer Wizard:

*1.* Close the table that you want to analyze, and display the Database window.

*2.* If the Analyze button looks like the button in the margin, click it to run the Table Analyzer Wizard.

Otherwise, click the down arrow next to the Analyze button, and choose Analyze Table. Whichever method you use, Access displays the first Table Analyzer Wizard window, which contains an explanation of what the wizard does.

Click the arrow buttons if you want to see examples of why duplicated information can be a problem.

*3.* Click Next to view more explanation.

Click the arrow buttons if you want to see examples of why multiple tables can work better than one table with repeated information.

*4.* Click Next again to see the next window, where you tell Access which tables you want to analyze.

*5.* Select the table you want the wizard to work with and then click Next.

*6.* You can have the wizard split your table (leaving the original table intact, in case you don't like what the wizard does), or you can use the wizard to tell Access exactly how to split the table.

*7.* Click Next to see how the fields are split into different tables.

*8.* Correct any fields that the wizard may have placed in the wrong table by clicking and dragging the field to another table. If you chose to split the table yourself, create new tables by clicking and dragging fields.

**9.** Click <u>N</u>ext to see the next window. From this point on, you see different windows if you chose to split the table yourself.

**10.** If the wizard is splitting the table, it asks you to confirm that the fields displayed in bold uniquely identify each record in the table.

**11.** To have Access create a primary key for you, click the Set Unique Key button.

**12.** Click <u>N</u>ext to see the next window. Access may display additional windows, depending on the table that you are splitting. Continue answering the questions until you see the Finish flag on the last window.

**13.** The last window enables you to create a query that looks like your original table. Click the <u>Y</u>es, create the query radio button to create that query.

You can also use the Display <u>H</u>elp on working with the new tables or query check box to get immediate help with your new creations.

**14.** Click <u>F</u>inish to create the new tables and close the Table Analyzer Wizard.

# Queries: Getting Answers from Your Data

Queries are the Access feature that enables you to view subsets of your data. You can use a query to view information from more than one table (when the tables are linked). You can use queries to view a subset of information — perhaps you want to view account information for only the accounts that are overdue. You can even use queries to create new calculated fields.

Part IV explains how to create queries to get information from one table or several tables. This part also explains how to phrase your questions so that you get the answer you're looking for.

## In this part . . .

- ✔ Using queries to create calculated fields
- ✔ Creating action queries
- ✔ Creating crosstab queries
- ✔ Creating select queries
- ✔ Using wizards to create queries
- ✔ Using criteria in queries
- ✔ Using the Query by Example (QBE) grid

# *About Queries*

Queries enable you to pull specific data from one or more tables into a datasheet. Access determines which fields and records to display in the new datasheet by using the query grid in the Query Design view.

Like tables, queries have two views: Design view and Datasheet view. In the Design view, you tell Access from which tables you want to see fields, which fields you want to see, and the criteria that have to be true for a record to appear on the resulting datasheet. *Criteria* are tests that a record has to pass — for example, you may want to see only records that have a value in the Amount field that is greater than 100. The criterion is that the value in the Amount field must be greater than 100.

In Datasheet view, you see the fields and records that Access has found that meet your criteria.

A query doesn't store data — it just pulls data out of tables for you to look at. A query is *dynamic* — as you add to or change your data, the result of the query also changes. When you save your query, you're not saving the table that the query produces — you're just saving the query design so that you can ask the same question again.

Following are some kinds of queries:

✦ **Advanced filter/sort:** The Advanced Filter/Sort feature in Access is the simplest kind of query; it allows you to find and sort information from one table in the database.

✦ **Select:** A select query finds the data you want from one or more tables and displays it in the order in which you want it displayed. A select query can include criteria that tell Access to filter records and display only some of them.

✦ **Total:** These queries are similar to select queries, but they allow you to calculate a sum or some other aggregate (such as an average).

✦ **Action:** Action queries change your data based on some set of criteria. Action queries can delete records, update data, append data from one or more tables to another table, and make a new table.

✦ **Crosstab:** Most tables in Access, including ones generated by queries, have records down the side and field names across the top. Crosstab queries produce tables with the values from one field down the side and values from another field across the top of the table. A crosstab query performs a calculation — it sums, averages, or counts data that is categorized in two ways.

# Asking Questions in Query Design View

Whichever kind of query you're using, you have to use Query Design view to tell Access about the data you're looking for and where Access should look for it.

Do one of the following to display a query in Design view:

✦ Select the query name on the Queries tab of the Database window and click <u>D</u>esign.

✦ Ctrl+double-click the query name in the Database window.

Query by Example (QBE) pane —

Tables used in query ──────────────── Pane divider —

Field names ──── Table names ──── Table pane —

The following table explains what the buttons on the Query Design view toolbar do.

| Toolbar Button | Button Name | What It Does |
| --- | --- | --- |
| | View | Displays Datasheet view |
| | Save | Saves the query so that you can view the design and the query datasheet again |
| | Undo | Undoes your last undoable action (Many actions cannot be undone, so keeping a backup is always a good idea.) |

*(continued)*

| Toolbar Button | Button Name | What It Does |
|---|---|---|
| | Select Query Type | Displays a drop-down list from which you can choose a query type: Select Query, Crosstab Query, Make-Table Query, Update Query, Append Query, or Delete Query |
| | Run | Runs the query (For a select query, clicking the Run button does the same thing as clicking the View button. When the query is an action query, the Run button performs the action. Use this button carefully.) |
| | Show Table | Displays the Show Table dialog box so that you can add tables to the query |
| | Totals | Displays the Total row in the query grid (Use the total row to tell Access what kind of calculation you want.) |
| All | Top Values | Limits the result of the query displayed in the datasheet to the number of records or the percentage of records displayed in this option |
| | Properties | Displays properties for the selected field or field list |
| | Build | Displays the Expression Builder dialog box (This button is "live" only when the cursor is in the Field or Criteria row.) |
| | Database Window | Displays the Database window |

The top half of the window displays the tables that you want to use in the query. Use the bottom half of the window to give Access specifics about the datasheet that the query will produce (what fields to display, how to decide whether to display a record, and so on).

Each row in the query grid has a specific purpose. Here's how to use each of them:

| Query Grid Row | What It Does |
|---|---|
| Field | Provides the name of a field that you want to include in a query |
| Table | Provides the name of the table that the field comes from (This row is not always visible.) |
| Total | Performs calculations in your query (This row is not always visible — use the Totals button on the toolbar to display or hide it.) |
| Sort | Determines the sort order of the datasheet produced by the query |

| Query Grid Setting | What It Does |
|---|---|
| Show | Shows a field (If you want to use a field to determine which records should be displayed on the datasheet, but not actually display the field, remove the check mark from the Show column for the field.) |
| Criteria | Tells Access the criteria for the field in the same column |
| Or | Adds OR criteria |

## Changing the size of query panes

You can change the size of the panes in Query view by clicking and dragging the pane divider. Just move the mouse pointer to the divider, where it changes shape; then click and drag to move the divider.

## Changing the size of tables in the table pane

The tables in the table pane are really just little windows — you can move and size them in the same way that you move and size windows. Change the size by moving the mouse pointer to the border of the window, where it turns into a double-headed arrow; then click and drag the border to change the size of the window. (To move a table in the table pane, click and drag its title bar.)

## Navigating Query Design view

You can work in Query Design view by using the mouse (to click the pane that you want) and the scroll bars (to see parts of the view that don't fit on the screen). But if you prefer, you can use the keyboard to move around.

The following keys move you around Query Design view:

| Key | What It Does in the Table Pane | What It Does in the Query Pane |
|---|---|---|
| F6 | Switches to the other pane | Switches to the other pane |
| Tab | Moves to the next table | Moves to the next row to the right |
| Alt+↓ | Nothing | Displays the drop-down list (if the row has one) |
| PgDn | Displays more field names in the active table | Displays more OR criteria |
| Home | Moves to the top of field names | Moves to the first column in the grid |

# Attaching a Table to a Query

It's a little odd that to add a table to a query, you use a dialog box called Show Table — but that's how it's done. Display the Show Table dialog box by doing any of the following things:

✦ Right-click the table part of Query Design view and choose Show Table from the shortcut menu

 ✦ Click the Show Table button

✦ Choose Query➪Show Table

After you display the Show Table dialog box, you add a table to the table pane of Query Design view by doing either of the following things:

✦ Double-clicking the table name in the Show Table dialog box

✦ Selecting the table and then clicking the Add button

You can also add a query to the table pane if you want to use a field that was created or filtered by a query. Click the appropriate tab at the top of the Show Table dialog box to see all Tables, all Queries, or all tables and queries (Both).

When you have added all the tables that you need, click the Close button in the Show Table dialog box to work with the Query window.

To remove a table from a query, press Delete when a field in the table is highlighted. Deleting a table from a query is absurdly easy and can have damaging consequences for your query — when a table is deleted, all the fields from that table are deleted from the query grid. Take care when your fingers get close to the Delete key.

# Calculating a Group of Data (Aggregate Calculations)

When you want to create a calculation that works with a group of data, you need an aggregate calculation. For example, you may want to count the number of orders that come in each day, or calculate an average amount for all orders.

When you create an aggregate calculation, you tell Access to *group* data using a particular field. For example, if you want to know the number of orders that come in each day, you need to group the order data by date, that is, using the field that contains the date. If you want to count the number of orders for each item, then you need to group using the field that contains the item name or number.

The easiest way to create aggregate calculations is to use the Summary option in the Simple Query Wizard. *See also* "Creating a Select Query," in this part.

## Using the Total row

The Total row in the query grid enables you to aggregate data. To perform a total calculation on your data, you must select one of the options from the drop-down list for each field in the query grid.

Σ The first step in creating a total is displaying the Total row in the query grid by clicking the Totals button. The Totals button appears to be raised when the Total row is not displayed and depressed when the Total row is displayed (you have to move the pointer to the button to see the 3-D effect).

The following table lists the choices for the Total row and how each works:

| Total Row | How It Works |
|---|---|
| Group By | Groups the values in this field so that like values are in the same group, allowing you to perform calculations on a group |
| Sum | Calculates the sum (total) of values in the field |
| Avg | Calculates the average of values in the field |
| Min | Finds the minimum value in the field |
| Max | Finds the maximum value in the field |
| Count | Counts the entries in the field (does not count blanks) |
| StDev | Calculates the standard deviation of values in the field |
| Var | Calculates the variance of values in the field |
| First | Finds the value in the first record in the field |
| Last | Finds the value in the last record in the field |
| Expression | Tells Access that you plan to type your own expression for the calculation |
| Where | Tells Access to use the field to limit the data included in the total calculation |

## Calculating aggregates for all records

If you don't use the Group By option for any of the fields included in the query grid, the result of any aggregation is the same — the "group" that you're aggregating includes all records.

Each field with an aggregate function (Sum, Avg, Min, Max, Count, StDev, Var, First, or Last) in the Total row is displayed as a calculated field in the datasheet that results from the query. The following query design:

produces this datasheet:

Access creates new fields to hold the aggregate calculation. You can use these new fields in reports, forms, and other queries.

## Calculating aggregates on groups of records

The Group By option in the Total row enables you to perform an aggregate calculation on a group of records. For example, if you want to calculate income received for each type of item sold, you need to group by the field that contains the item name or number, and then sum the field containing the amount each item sold for. The result is a datasheet that has one row for each type of item (with no repetitions) and a calculated field with the sum of income for that item.

To create an aggregate calculation for grouped records, follow these steps:

*1.* Create a new query in Design view.

*See also* "Creating a Select Query," in this part.

*2.* From the Show Tables window, choose the tables that you need fields from and add them to the query. Close the Show Tables window.

*3.* Move the field that you want to group data by into the query grid.

*4.* Choose Group By from the drop-down list in the Total row.

If the Total row doesn't appear in the query grid, click the Totals button on the toolbar.

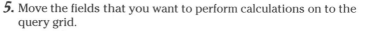

**5.** Move the fields that you want to perform calculations on to the query grid.

**6.** Choose the type of calculation that you want for each field from the drop-down list in the Total row.

If you want to perform more than one kind of calculation on a field, put the field into several columns in the query grid. For example, if you want to count the number of calls and sum the total minutes spent on calls, you may put the Call Minutes field into two columns in the query grid and choose Sum in the Total row of one of the Call Minutes columns and Count in the Total row of the other Call Minutes column.

To perform more than one type of calculation on a field, put the field in more than one column in the query grid and specify a different type of calculation in each Total row.

For example, this query:

```
Query1 : Select Query                                          _ □ ×

   Items ordered          Order Summary
   Item Descripti ▲        *
   Item Number      1      Order ID
   Number of iter          Catalog
   Cost per item           Shipping
   Shipping       ▼   ∞    Date


  Field:  Catalog        ▼  Item ID            Number of items    Cost per item
  Table:  Order Summary     Items ordered      Items ordered      Items ordered
  Total:  Group By          Count              Max                Avg
  Sort:
  Show:        ☑                  ☑                  ☑                  ☑
  Criteria:
  or:
```

produces this datasheet:

```
Query1 : Select Query                                               _ □ ×
        Catalog        CountOfItem ID   MaxOfNumber of items   AvgOfCost per item
▶  Crate & Barrel   ▼               2                      1            $136.98
   Harry and David                  3                      1             $31.62
   Hold everything                  4                      1             $50.25
   J. Crew                          4                      1             $34.50
   Lands End                        6                      2             $50.33
   Williams-Sonoma                  5                      1             $38.20


  Record:  ◄◄  ◄            1  ►  ►I ►*  of 6
```

You can also group by more than one field. If you want aggregate information about people who have the same last name and live at the same address, you can use the Group By setting in both the last name field and the address field.

### Limiting the records to aggregate

You can use the Criteria and the Total rows together to limit the records that are used in the aggregate calculation or to limit the records displayed after the calculations are performed.

You have to be careful, though, to make sure that Access does exactly what you want it to do. Here are some tips on using the Criteria and Total rows in one query.

✦ If you use Criteria in a Group By field, you limit the data that Access uses for the aggregate calculation. In other words, Access first finds the records that meet the criterion and then performs the aggregate calculation with just those records.

✦ If you use Criteria in a field with an aggregate function (Sum, Avg, Min, Max, Count, StDev, Var, First, or Last), Access first does the calculation and then includes the records that meet the criteria in the datasheet.

✦ Use the Where option in the Total row when you want to limit the records used for the calculation by using a field that is not a Group By field. When you use the Where option, you can also use a criterion. The Where option limits the records used for the aggregate calculation to those that pass the criterion for the field — think of it as meaning "Limit the records to Where this criterion is true."

When you use the Where option, you use it only to limit records — Access knows this and turns off the Show checkbox. In fact, you can't show a field used with the Where option in the Total row. If you want to display a field used with the Where option, use the same field in another column of the query grid with the Group By option in the Total row.

### Creating your own expression for an aggregate calculation

You're not limited to the aggregate functions Access provides to perform a calculation in a query — you can write your own expression, instead. To write your own expression for the aggregate calculation, choose Expression in the Total row and type the expression into the Field row of the grid.

To create your own expression, follow these steps:

*1.* Move your cursor to the Field row of a blank column in the query grid.

*2.* Type the name of the new field that you are creating, followed by a colon.

**3.** Type the expression in the Field row after the colon.

**4.** Select Expression in the Total row of the new field.

*See also* "Calculating Fields (Building Expressions)," in this part, for more information on creating expressions.

# Calculating Fields (Building Expressions)

When you're creating your database, don't waste your time dragging out your calculator, doing the math yourself, and then typing in the result. Instead, tell Access to perform any calculations for you. The work gets done faster, and the result is always up to date — even if you later add, delete, or change records.

You can add calculations to queries and reports by typing an expression, sometimes called a *formula,* that tells Access exactly what to calculate. In a query, you put the expression in one column of the Field row of the query grid.

Most expressions include some basic elements, such as field names, values, and operators. Field names must be enclosed in brackets. Here's an example of an expression that you might use to calculate profit when you have fields called Revenues and Expenses:

```
Profit: [Revenues] - [Expenses]
```

You can also use values in an expression, as follows:

```
Retail Cost: [Wholesale Cost] *1.50
```

You aren't limited to performing calculations with values; you can also perform calculations with dates, times, and text data. *See* "Using functions," later in this section, for more information on working with non-numeric data.

Some types of data must be enclosed between special characters so that Access knows what kind of data it is. The following table tells you how to use different elements in an expression:

| Type of Data in an Expression | How It Should Look |
| --- | --- |
| Text | "Massachusetts" |
| Date/time | #15-jan-97# |
| Field name | [Cost] |

The following are the basic steps to take to add a calculated field to a query:

*1.* Create a new query.

*2.* Include all the tables that have fields that you want to use in a calculation.

*3.* In the query grid, click the Field row of a blank column.

*4.* Type the name of the new field, followed by a colon.

If you don't give the new field a name, Access names it for you — with something unintelligible, such as Expr1 (for Expression 1). If you're writing an expression to calculate cost and you want to call the new field Total Cost, type: **Total Cost:**

*5.* Type the expression that you want Access to calculate.

In the following query, the new field is called Total Cost, and the expression to calculate Total Cost follows the colon.

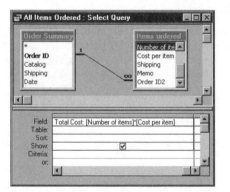

 *6.* To see the result, click the View button.

After you create the new field, you can use it in other queries and in other calculations.

> **TIP** Access won't make the column in the query grid wider just because you're typing a great deal of text in it. You may want to make the column wider so that you can see its contents — at least until you're sure that the calculation is working. After that, you can make the column narrow again. *See also* "Changing Column Width," in Part III.

## Using a parameter in an expression

You may want to change the value in an expression without having to rewrite the expression in Query Design view each time. You can do so by referring to a field name that doesn't actually exist in the expression that you create. When you ask to view the query's datasheet, Access displays the Enter Parameter Value dialog box and tells you the name of the field for which it needs a value.

Enter the value of the field name listed, and click OK to see the datasheet.

## Changing the format of a calculated field

To change the format of a calculated field, follow these steps:

**1.** In Query Design view, right-click anywhere in the column that contains the field you want to format.

**2.** Choose Properties from the shortcut menu.

Access displays the Field Properties dialog box.

**3.** Display the drop-down list for Format to display the format options.

**4.** Choose the format option that you want from the drop-down list.

The options in the Field Properties dialog box are exactly the same as the options that appear in the Field Properties pane of Table Design view, and you can use them in exactly the same way. *See also* "Customizing Fields Using the Field Properties Pane," in Part III.

## Using operators in calculations

Access has a slew of operators. The operators that you're most likely to have worked with are the *logical* and *relational* operators, which result in a true or false result. However, Access also has operators that you use in calculations.

*Mathematical operators* work with numbers. The following table lists mathematical operators and what they do.

| Mathematical Operator | What It Does |
|---|---|
| * | Multiplies |
| + | Adds |
| − | Subtracts |
| / | Divides |
| \ | Divides the rounded integer values and produces a rounded integer value; can be used to calculate an integer value (n\1) |
| ^ | Raises to a power |

Text data is often called a *string* by technoids. Text/string operators work with text and memo fields. You can add two strings together by using &, the string operator that concatenates strings. There are also functions that work with strings.

You can concatenate different sorts of data in an expression; you're not limited to text data. You may want to include a numeric value or a date in a string, for example. Using the & operator converts data to a string, so the final result is a string.

## Using functions

Functions allow you to create calculations that would be difficult or impossible to perform with operators. The following are the six major categories of functions that you're likely to use:

+ **Conversion:** Convert one type of data to another (numeric to string, for example).

+ **Date/Time:** Work with time and date data.

+ **Financial:** Perform financial calculations.

+ **Mathematical:** Perform mathematical calculations.

+ **Text:** Manipulate text or string expressions.

+ **Domain:** Calculate aggregate statistics on a set of records.

All functions are used in a similar way — use the name of the function followed by the argument or arguments in parentheses. *Arguments* are what the function uses to perform its calculation. The function Sqr( ), for example, takes the square root of a number, so the following expression would produce the square root of the value in the field called Hypotenuse:

```
SQR([Hypotenuse])
```

Remember that the argument has to be enclosed in parentheses, and a field name used in an expression has to be enclosed in square brackets. For the rules on using field names, dates, and strings in expressions, *see* the introduction to this topic, "Calculating Fields (Building Expressions)."

The best way to see the Access functions and to use them in building expressions is to use the Functions folder in the Expression Builder.

## *Using the Expression Builder*

When you know what you want your expression to do, but you're not sure how to write it so that Access understands it, you may find the Expression Builder useful. The Expression Builder can help you avoid errors in an expression, but it can't help you figure out how to create the calculation you need. Your formulas will look just as complicated in the Expression Builder as they will when you type them directly in the Field row of the query grid.

To use the Expression Builder to write a calculation, follow these steps:

*1.* Click the Field row in the column where you want to add a calculation.

 *2.* Click the Build button in the toolbar.

Access displays the Expression Builder.

Objects contained in object selected in first box

┌Operators you can click | Expression box

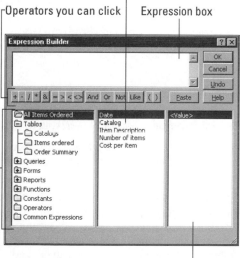

└Database objects

More detail about items selected in first two boxes

The Build button is unavailable (grayed out) except when the cursor is in a Field row or a Criteria row — the only two rows in the query grid where an expression is allowed. (You can use the Expression Builder to build a Criteria expression as well as to build an expression for a calculated field.)

The Expression Builder allows you to choose field names, operators, and parentheses (to determine the order of calculation) to build an expression. The Expression Builder takes care of the funny characters that Access needs in an expression, such as the square brackets around field names. The Expression Builder also lists all of Access's operators and functions, so that you don't have to type them yourself and risk typos. But using the Expression Builder is not for the faint of heart — you may find typing simple expressions directly into the query grid easier than trying to figure out all the boxes in the Expression Builder.

Here are some ways to use the Expression Builder:

✦ You can type directly in the Expression box — just click it and start typing.

✦ You can put operators in the Expression box by clicking the button that shows the operator you want to use in your expression.

✦ You can put an element from the lower boxes in the Expression box by double-clicking it or by highlighting it and then clicking the Paste button.

✦ You can undo the last thing that you did to the expression by clicking the Undo button.

✦ When you add a field name from a lower box to the expression, Access includes the name of the table that the field comes from, as follows:

```
[table name]![field name]
```

✦ You can expand any folder with a plus sign (+; these folders appear in the first lower box) by double-clicking it.

✦ When you click an object (such as a table, query, form, or report name), the names of the fields used in that object appear in the second lower box.

✦ If you put the names of two fields in the Expression box without an operator between them, Access adds a generic operator (<<Expr>>). To put a real operator in the expression, select the generic operator and then click an operator button. Access replaces <<Expr>> with the operator that you clicked.

✦ All Access functions are available from the Expression Builder. Double-click the Functions folder in the first lower box and then click Built-in Functions. Access displays categories of functions in the second box. Click a category to see specific functions in the third box. Click a function; Access displays an example of how it should be used at the bottom of the dialog box.

✦ Access provides some common expressions in the Common Expressions folder, which appears at the bottom of the first box.

# *Correcting a Query*

You can do a few things in a query to make it even better — you can move the columns around, delete a column, or delete all the entries in the design grid.

To do any of those things, though, you first have to select the column in the grid by clicking the column selector — the gray block at the top of each column in the grid.

Column selector

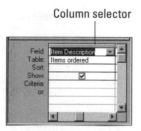

Here are some things you may want to do to make your query better:

| When You Want to . . . | Here's What to Do |
| --- | --- |
| Move a column | Click the column selector to select the column, click a second time, and then drag the column to its new position. |
| Delete a column | Click the column selector to select the column; then press the Delete key to delete the column. |
| Delete all columns | Choose Edit⇨Clear Grid. |
| Insert a column | Drag a field from the table pane to the column in the grid where you want to insert it. Access inserts an extra column for the new field. |
| Change the displayed name | Use a colon between the display name and the actual name of the field in the Field row (*display name:field name*). |

# Creating Action Queries

*Action queries* are a way to make a global correction to your database. Before you delve into the complexities of action queries, though, you should consider whether you can fix the problem by using the much simpler Find dialog box to find and replace data. *See* "Finding Data in a Table," in Part III, for more information on the Find dialog box.

Action queries differ significantly from select queries, which are the kind that you'll use most often. A select query shows you data that meet your criteria; an action query does something with the data that meet your criteria.

You may need to create an action query if you want to do any of the following things:

+ Delete some records *(delete query)*.

+ Append data from one table to another table *(append query)*.

+ Update information in some records *(update query)*.

+ Create a new table from data stored in other tables *(make-table query)*.

When you create a query by choosing Design View in the New Query dialog box (*see* "Creating a Select Query" for more information), Access automatically creates a select query.

To change the query type, do either of the following things:

+ Click the arrow next to the Query Type button and choose the query type that you want.

+ Choose the type of query you want from the Query menu. (You can choose Query⇨Make Table Query, Query⇨Update Query, Query⇨Append Query, or Query⇨Delete Query to create an action query.)

Use the View button and the Run button when you create action queries. When you work with a Select Query, the View and Run buttons do the same thing. When you work with an Action query, the View and Run buttons do completely different jobs:

+ The View button displays Datasheet view, which is a good way to preview what you're going to do with the action query.

+ The Run button executes the action — it deletes or changes data in your database. You cannot undo the action after you click the Run button in an action query, so be very sure that the query is set up correctly before you run it.

When you double-click an action query in the Database window or use another method to open a query, you're telling Access to run the query (not just to show it). Access warns you that you are about to do whatever it is you're about to do — update records, delete records, or whatever — and gives you a chance to renege. If all you want to do is work on the design of the query, make sure that you select the query and click the Design button.

It's easy to recognize action queries in the Database window, because their icons are a little different from the icons that select queries have — all action-query icons have an exclamation point.

You can avoid accidentally acting on the wrong record in two ways:

✦ The really safe method is to first create a select query, to ensure that the records that are selected are the records that you actually want to perform the action on.

✦ The fairly-safe-but-not-absolutely-foolproof method is to set up your query and then click the View button to see Datasheet view. The datasheet shows you the data that the query has found to act on. Be careful to use the View button rather than the Run button, which actually performs the action.

## Update queries

You can use an *update query* to change a pile of data at the same time — to raise prices by 10 percent, for example, or to change the earthquake risk of all your New Hampshire insurance clients from low to medium.

To create an update query, follow these steps:

*1.* Create a new query in Design view.

Access displays Query Design View and the Show Table dialog box.

*See also* "Creating a Select Query," in this part.

*2.* Add the tables that you plan to update or that you need to use fields from to establish the update criteria.

*3.* Close the Show Table dialog box.

*4.* Change the query type to Update Query by clicking the arrow next to the Query Type button and choosing Update Query from the drop-down list or by choosing Query⇨Update Query.

**5.** Put fields in the query grid.

Add fields that you want to see in the datasheet, that you want to use with criteria to tell Access exactly what to update, and that you actually want to update.

**6.** Add the criteria to tell Access how to choose the records to update.

**7.** Use the Update To row to tell Access how to update the data.

This query finds records where the state is equal to "NH" and changes the value of the field Earthquake Risk for those records to Medium.

The easiest update is to change one value to another by simply typing the new value in the Update To box. More complex updates include expressions that tell Access exactly how to update the field. You can use the Expression Builder to help you build an expression for the Update To setting; just click the Build button. *See also* "Calculating Fields (Building Expressions.)"

**8.** Click the View button.

Access displays the datasheet with the records the query found that match your criteria. If the data is not correct, return to Design view to correct the fields and criteria.

TIP

You can only display fields in the datasheet that the update query is actually working with; in an update query, every field displayed in the datasheet has either an expression in the Criteria row or a value or expression in the Update To row in the query grid. If you want to get a fuller picture of the records you're updating (see the data for all the fields, for example), you can change the query type back to Select, add additional fields, and view the datasheet that your criteria produces. When you change the query type back to Update, the Update To options you added will still be there. Don't forget to remove the additional fields from the query grid before you run the update.

 **9.** Run the update by clicking the Run button.

Access warns you that after the records are updated, you can't undo the changes.

Microsoft Access

⚠ You are about to update 8 row[s].

Once you click Yes, you can't use the Undo command to reverse the changes.
Are you sure you want to update these records?

[ Yes ]    [ No ]

**10.** Click Yes to update the data.

**11.** Check the tables with affected fields to see whether the update query worked correctly.

**12.** Delete the query if you won't be using it again; save it if you will need it again.

## Make-table queries

A *make-table query* can be useful if you need to make a new table to export or to serve as a backup. You can also simply make a copy of a table or query — *See* "Finding Your Way Around a Database," in Part II.

To create a table with a make-table query, follow these steps:

**1.** Create a new select query that produces the records you want in a new table. Access copies the records to the new table.

*See also* "Creating a Select Query," in this part.

 **2.** Change the query type to make-table by clicking the arrow next to the Query Type button and choosing Make Table Query from the drop-down list or by choosing Query⇨Make Table Query.

Access immediately displays the Make Table dialog box.

**3.** In the Table Name box, type the name of the table that you're creating.

**4.** Click OK.

Access displays Query Design view. A make-table query has the same rows in the query grid as a select query.

**5.** Click the View button to see the records that Access will copy to the new table. You may need to return to the Design view to edit the query until all the records you want in the new table appear in the datasheet when you click the View button.

**6.** Click the Run button to create the new table.

Access asks whether you're sure, because you won't be able to undo your changes.

**7.** Click Yes to create the new table.

**8.** Check the new and old tables to make sure that you got what you need in the new table.

## Append queries

An *append query* takes data from one or more tables or queries in your database and adds it to an existing table. As with other queries, you can use criteria to tell Access exactly which data to append.

Cutting and pasting is often an easier way to append records from one table to another. *See* "Cutting, Copying, and Pasting," in Part VIII, for more information.

Access gets a little picky about data that you append using an append query, especially when it comes to the primary key field. You must follow these rules when appending records to another table:

✦ Data that you want to append must have unique values in the field that is the primary key field in the table to which the data is being appended. If the field is blank, or if the same value already exists in the table, Access does not append the records.

✦ If the primary key field in the table to which the data is being appended is an AutoNumber field, do not append that field — Access generates new numbers in the AutoNumber field for the new records.

✦ The type of data in records that you're appending must match the type of data in the table to which you're appending them.

To create an append query, follow these steps:

**1.** Create a select query that produces the records that you want to add to another table.

   ***See also*** "Creating a Select Query," in this part.

 **2.** Change the query type to Append by clicking the arrow next to the Query Type button and choosing <u>A</u>ppend Query from the drop-down list or by choosing Query⇨<u>A</u>ppend Query.

   Access immediately displays the Append dialog box.

| Append | ? X |
|--------|-----|
| **Append To** | |
| Table <u>N</u>ame: [＿＿＿＿＿＿▼] | OK |
| | Cancel |
| ⦿ <u>C</u>urrent Database | |
| ○ <u>A</u>nother Database: | |
| <u>F</u>ile Name: [＿＿＿＿＿＿] | |

**3.** Choose the table to which you want to append the records.

   You can display the names of all the tables in the open database by displaying the Table <u>N</u>ame drop-down list.

   You can add the records to a table in another database, but you have to know the exact name of the database file, including the folder structure.

**4.** Click OK.

   Access returns you to the query design. The title bar of the Query Design view window tells you that you're working with an append query. The query grid has an extra row: the Append To row. Access automatically fills in the Append To row with the names of the fields in the table you're appending records to, if the field names match the names of the fields you're appending.

**5.** If some of the fields don't have field names in the Append To row, display the drop-down list in the Append row and select the name of the field you want to append to. When you're finished, check each column:

   • The Field row contains the name of the field that contains data that you want to append to another table.

   • The Table row contains the name of the table that contains the data.

   • The Append To row contains the name of the field that the data will be appended to.

**6.** Click the Run button to run the append query.

Access tells you that you're about to append rows and that you won't be able to undo the changes.

**7.** Click Yes to run the query.

Access adds the records to the table you specified. You now have the same information in two tables.

**8.** Save the query if you think that you'll use it again; otherwise, close it without saving.

**9.** Check your results.

Check the table you appended to as well as the table you were appending from to make sure that Access copied all the records that you wanted to copy.

## Delete queries

A *delete query* enables you to select your fields and add criteria in the same way that a select query does, but instead of displaying the records that the query finds, a delete query deletes them.

Delete queries are dangerous because they actually delete data from the tables in your database. Always make sure that you have a backup of your database's file before you run a delete query. *See* "Backing Up Your Database," in Part VIII, for more information.

When you tell Access to create a delete query, the Show row in the query grid is replaced by the Delete row. The Delete row has a drop-down list with two options:

✦ **Where:** Tells Access to use the criteria for the field to determine which records to delete.

✦ **From:** Displays the field when you view the datasheet for the query. You can choose the From option only when you use the * choice in the Field row to include all fields from a table. Viewing all fields from a table in the datasheet gives you a more complete picture of the data you're deleting; otherwise, all you see in the datasheet are the values from the fields that you include in the query grid with criteria.

Here's how to create a delete query:

**1.** In Design view, create a new query that produces the records you want to delete.

*See* "Creating a Select Query," in this part.

Access displays the Query Design view and the Show Tables dialog box.

**2.** Add to the query all tables that have data you want to delete.

**3.** Close the Show Tables dialog box.

**4.** Change the query type to Delete Query by clicking the down arrow next to the Query Type button and choosing <u>D</u>elete Query from the drop-down list or by choosing Query⇨<u>D</u>elete Query.

When you change the query type from select to delete, Access replaces the Sort row of the query grid with the Delete row.

**5.** Drag the asterisk from the first table to the query grid. Repeat for any other tables that you're using in the table grid.

Access puts the asterisk — the symbol for all fields from a table — in the query grid. Notice that the value in the Delete row is From. This value tells Access to display the fields in the datasheet but not to use them to determine the data to delete.

**6.** Put the fields that you will use to tell Access which records to delete in the query grid.

When you add a single field to the query grid, Access gives it the Where option in the Delete row. The delete query uses the Criteria row of fields with the Where option to determine which records to delete.

**7.** Type the criteria.

If you want to delete records in which the Cost Per Item field is greater than 100, for example, type **>100** in the Criteria row of the Cost Per Item column.

| | | |
|---|---|---|
| Field: Items ordered.* | Cost per item | |
| Table: Items ordered | Items ordered | |
| Delete: From | Where | |
| Criteria: | >100 | |
| or: | | |

Delete items over $100 : Delete Query

Items ordered
*
**Item ID**
Item Descripti...
Item Number
Number of ite...

**8.** Click the View button to see the records that the delete query will delete when you run it.

If you see data in the datasheet that shouldn't be deleted, or if data that you want to delete is missing, you need to correct the design of the query before you run it. Remember that a delete query deletes entire records.

**9.** Return to Design view by clicking the View button.

**10.** Run the query by clicking the Run button.

Access deletes the data that you saw in Datasheet view — and it's gone for good!

You can delete records from related tables, but the relationships must be defined, and you need to check two options in the Relationships dialog box for each specific join: the Enforce Referential Integrity option and the Cascade Delete Related Fields option. Display the Relationships dialog box by double-clicking the line that connects two tables in Relationships view. *See also* "Relating (Linking) Tables," in Part II.

# Creating a Crosstab Query

A *crosstab query* is a specialized kind of query for displaying aggregated data. Instead of creating a table with rows showing record data and columns showing fields, you can use a crosstab query table to use data from one field for the row labels and data from another field for column labels. The result is a more compact, spreadsheetlike presentation of your data.

*See also* "Calculating a Group of Data (Aggregate Calculations)," in this part.

You may have a table in which Date and Class Level information are repeated, as shown in the following figure.

| Date | Class Level | Time | # attendees |
|------|-------------|------|-------------|
| 9/15/96 | Beginner | 9:00:00 AM | 9 |
| 9/15/96 | Intermediate | 1:00:00 PM | 5 |
| 9/15/96 | Advanced | 3:00:00 PM | 5 |
| 9/15/96 | Intermediate | 5:00:00 PM | 8 |
| 9/22/96 | Beginner | 9:00:00 AM | 8 |
| 9/22/96 | Intermediate | 1:00:00 PM | 4 |
| 9/29/96 | Beginner | 9:00:00 AM | 5 |
| 9/29/96 | Intermediate | 1:00:00 PM | 7 |
| 9/29/96 | Advanced | 3:00:00 PM | 8 |
| 10/6/96 | Beginner | 9:00:00 AM | 15 |
| 10/6/96 | Intermediate | 1:00:00 PM | 6 |
| 10/6/96 | Beginner | 5:00:00 PM | 7 |
| 10/20/96 | Beginner | 9:00:00 AM | 17 |
| 10/20/96 | Intermediate | 1:00:00 PM | 10 |
| 10/20/96 | Advanced | 3:00:00 PM | 7 |
| 10/27/96 | Beginner | 9:00:00 AM | 16 |
| 10/27/96 | Intermediate | 1:00:00 PM | 11 |
| 11/3/96 | Beginner | 9:00:00 AM | 10 |
| 11/3/96 | Intermediate | 1:00:00 PM | 9 |
| 11/3/96 | Advanced | 3:00:00 PM | 9 |

Record: 1 of 37

A crosstab query enables you to see this information in a more compact form, with the dates being the row labels, and the class levels being the column labels.

| Classes_Crosstab1 : Crosstab Query | | | |
|---|---|---|---|
| Date | Beginner | Intermediate | Advanced |
| 9/15/96 | 9 | 13 | 5 |
| 9/22/96 | 8 | 4 | |
| 9/29/96 | 5 | 7 | 8 |
| 10/6/96 | 22 | 6 | |
| 10/20/96 | 17 | 10 | 7 |
| 10/27/96 | 16 | 11 | |
| 11/3/96 | 10 | 9 | 9 |
| 11/10/96 | 11 | 5 | |
| 11/17/96 | 15 | 16 | |
| 11/24/96 | 16 | 12 | |
| 12/1/96 | 12 | 8 | 5 |
| 12/8/96 | 11 | 9 | |
| 12/15/96 | 22 | 11 | |
| 12/22/96 | 11 | 10 | |

Record: 1 of 14

## Using Query Design view

A simple crosstab query has three fields — one used for row head-ings (Date, for example), one used for column headings (Class Level, for example), and one used to fill up the table (number of students, for example). The third field is called the Value field, and you can tell Access how to summarize your data in the crosstab table by choos-ing from these choices: Sum, Avg, Min, Max, Count, StDev, Var, First, or Last. *See also* "Calculating a Group of Data (Aggregate Calcula-tions)," in this part, for more information on aggregating fields.

Here's how to create a simple crosstab query:

*1.* Display the Queries tab of the Database window and click the New button.

Access displays the New Query window.

*2.* Select Design View from the New Query window and click OK.

Access displays the Query Design view and the Show Table dialog box.

*3.* Double-click the tables or queries you want to use to create the crosstab query to add them to the table pane of the Design view.

*See also* "Creating a Select Query," in this part.

*4.* Close the Show table dialog box.

*5.* Change the query type to Crosstab by clicking the arrow next to the Query Type button and choosing Crosstab Query from the drop-down list.

You can also choose Query⇨Crosstab Query.

Access displays an additional row called Crosstab in the query grid. You use the Crosstab row to tell Access how to build the crosstab table.

**6.** Put the field that you want Access to use for row labels in the grid by double-clicking it.

**7.** Display the Crosstab options for the field by clicking the down arrow in the Crosstab row. Choose Row Heading from the drop-down list.

**8.** Put the field that you want Access to use for column labels in the grid by double-clicking it.

**9.** Display the Crosstab options for the field by clicking the down arrow in the Crosstab row. Choose Column Heading from the drop-down list.

**10.** Double-click the field that contains the values you want aggregated in your crosstab query to put it in the grid. This is the field that provides the values that fill up the crosstab table.

**11.** Display the Crosstab options for the field by clicking the down arrow in the Crosstab row. Choose Value from the drop-down list.

**12.** In the column that contains the Value field, choose the option to summarize the data from the drop-down list in the Total row. *See also* "Calculating a Group of Data (Aggregate Calculations)," in this part, for more information on the options in the Total row.

When you finish, your Query Design view should look something like this:

### Using the Crosstab Query Wizard

The Crosstab Query Wizard provides an automated way to create a crosstab query.

The Crosstab Query Wizard works only with one table or query. If the fields that you want to use in the crosstab query are not in one table, you have to create a query that combines those fields in one query before you use the Crosstab Query Wizard.

Start the Crosstab Query Wizard by following these steps:

*1.* Display the Queries tab of the Database window.

Access displays the names of any queries that you have in your database.

*2.* Click the New button.

Access displays the New Query dialog box.

*3.* Select Crosstab Query Wizard and click OK.

Access starts the Crosstab Query Wizard.

The Crosstab Query Wizard works like other wizards; it asks you questions in the form of dialog-box options. To see the next wizard screen, click the Next button. To go back to the preceding screen, click the Back button. *See also* "Working with Wizards," in Part I.

The Crosstab Query Wizard asks you for the following information:

✦ The table or query that you want to use to create the crosstab table

✦ The field that you want to use for row headings

✦ The field that you want to use for column headings

✦ The field that you want to summarize by using the row and column headings

✦ How you want to summarize the field (count the entries, add them together, average them, and so on)

✦ Whether you want Access to sum each row (Access adds a Sum of *field name* column to the table to display the result)

## Creating a Select Query

An ordinary query (one that displays fields based on the contents of a query grid) is called a *select query*. A select query is similar to the Advanced Filter/Sort, but has some additional features:

✦ A query shows only the fields that you tell it to show.

✦ You can use more than one table in a query.

✦ You can use fields from another query.

✦ Queries have some options that the Advanced Filter/Sort feature doesn't. You can show or hide the fields that you use in a query, and you can tell Access to show just the top *x* values when you use a query.

## Creating a select query from scratch

Here's how to create a select query from scratch:

***1.*** Display the Queries tab of the Database window.

***2.*** Click the New button.

Access displays the New Query dialog box. Select Design View if Access hasn't done so for you.

***3.*** Click OK.

Access displays Query Design view and the Show Table dialog box.

***4.*** Select the table(s) that contain fields you want to display in the query datasheet or use to create criteria by selecting the table(s) and then clicking the Add button in the Show Table dialog box.

If you want to include a field generated by another query, you can add queries to a query by clicking the Queries or Both tab of the Show Table dialog box and double-clicking the query name.

***5.*** Click the Close button in the Show Table dialog box.

***6.*** Select the fields that you want to use in the query table.

You can drag a field name to the design grid or double-click a field name to move it to the design grid. You can also use the drop-down Field and Table lists in the query grid to select the fields that you want to use.

**7.** Type the criteria that you want to use to create the query table.

For example, if you want to see only records with values in the Order Numbers field over 100, type **>100** in the Criteria row of the column that contains Order Numbers in a Field row. Or, if you want to see only records where the value of the Author field is Hemingway, type **Hemingway** in the Criteria row for the Author column.

***See also*** "Calculating a Group of Data (Aggregate Calculations)" in this part.

**8.** Set the Sort and Show options to create your perfect query table.

***See also*** "Asking Questions in Query Design View," in this part, for more information on using the Sort and Show rows in the query grid.

 **9.** Click the View button to view the results of the query in a datasheet.

**10.** Save the query by clicking the Save button in the query's Design or Datasheet view.

 If you are querying just one table, the easiest way to create the query is to select the table in the Database window and then click the New Object: Query button. (Query is not always what the New Object button is set to create — you may have to use the New Object button's drop-down list to choose Query.) Then select Design View in the New Query dialog box. Access displays Query Design view with the table that you selected displayed.

## Using the Simple Query Wizard

The Simple Query Wizard does a great deal of the work of creating a query for you. The most basic query that you can create with the Simple Query Wizard pulls together related data from different fields. The Simple Query Wizard is a terrific way to create some summary calculations from your data — such as how much was spent on an order or how many Items were ordered.

The Simple Query Wizard gives you the option of creating a *summary* or *detail* query if the fields you've chosen for the query include:

✦ A field with values

✦ A field with repetitions, used to group the values

A *detail query* lists every record that meets your criteria. A *summary query* performs calculations on your data to summarize it. You can sum, average, count the number of values in a field, or find the minimum or maximum value in a field. A summary query creates new calculated fields that you can use in other queries or in reports.

For example, if you have a field that lists the amount spent and a field that lists the dates on which the money was spent, Access can create a summary query for you that sums the amount spent by date.

This wizard works like all wizards — it displays screens in which you give it information. *See* "Working with Wizards," in Part I.

Follow these steps to use the Simple Query Wizard to create a query:

*1.* Create a new query by displaying the Queries tab of the Database Window and clicking New.

Access displays the New Query dialog box.

*2.* Select Simple Query Wizard and click OK.

Access displays the first window of the query.

*3.* Use the Tables/Queries list box to choose the first table or query that you want to use fields from.

When you select a table or query, fields from that object appear in the Available Fields list box.

*4.* Move fields you want to use in the query from the Available Fields list to the Selected Fields list by double-clicking a field name or by selecting the field name and then clicking the right-arrow button.

*5.* If you're using fields from more than one table or query, repeat Steps 3 and 4 to add fields from the additional tables or queries to the Selected Fields list.

*6.* Click Next when you have selected all the fields you need for the query.

Access displays the next window, which asks you if you want a
Detail or Summary query. If summary calculations are not possible
with the fields you've chosen, Access will skip this window.

**7.** Choose the type of query you want: Detail or Summary.

If you choose a Summary query, click the Summary Options
button to display the window where you tell the wizard how to
summarize each field.

Use the check boxes to indicate the new fields that Access
should create with this query. For example, if you want to add
the values in the Cost per item field, click the Sum check box in
the row for the Cost per item field.

| Summary Options | | | | | | |
|---|---|---|---|---|---|---|
| What summary values would you like calculated? | | | | | OK | |
| Field | Sum | Avg | Min | Max | Cancel | |
| Number of items | ☐ | ☐ | ☐ | ☐ | | |
| Cost per item | ☑ | ☐ | ☐ | ☐ | | |
| | | | | | ☐ Count records in Items ordered | |

Don't overlook the Count check boxes that may appear in this
window — selecting this box tells the wizard to create a field that
counts the records within each grouping.

**8.** Click OK to leave the Summary Options window.

**9.** Click Next to view the next window.

If you are summarizing data, and if the fields being summarized
can be grouped by a Time/Date field, the wizard displays a
window where you choose the time interval that the records
should be grouped by.

For example, if you have chosen to sum a field that details check
amounts, and check amounts were entered in a record that also
contained a field telling the date each check was written, you can
choose to display total check amounts by Day, Month, Quarter,
or Year. Select the time interval to group by.

**10.** Click Next to see the final window.

**11.** Type a name for the query in the box at the top of the window.

**12.** Choose whether you want to <u>O</u>pen the query to view information, which shows you the query in Datasheet view, or <u>M</u>odify the query design, which shows you the query in Design view.

If you want to see the help screen on working with a query, click the Display <u>H</u>elp on working with the query check box.

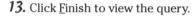

**13.** Click <u>F</u>inish to view the query.

You can't tell the Simple Query Wizard about criteria. If you want to include criteria in your query, open the query in Design view and add the criteria.

*See also* "Limiting Records with Criteria Expressions" in this part.

## Displaying or Hiding Table Names

You can view table names for each field in the query grid, or you can choose not to see the Table row.

To make the Table row appear or disappear, do either of the following things:

✦ Right-click the grid and choose Table <u>N</u>ames from the shortcut menu.

✦ Choose <u>V</u>iew⇨Table <u>N</u>ames (to turn off the check mark).

## Filtering Only One Table with Advanced Filter/Sort

The easiest kind of query to create is one that filters records in only one table. You perform this simple query by using the Advanced Filter/Sort command.

Follow these steps:

**1.** Open the table you want to filter in Datasheet view.

**2.** Choose <u>R</u>ecords⇨<u>F</u>ilter⇨<u>A</u>dvanced Filter/Sort.

Access displays the Filter window, which has two parts, just like the Query Design view. *See also* "Asking Questions in Query Design View" in this part.

Table you're querying          Design grid where you build your query

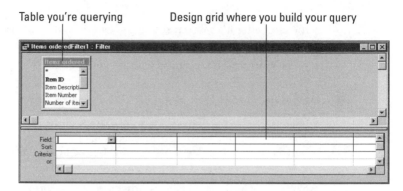

**3.** Click the first field that you want to use to filter the table and drag it to the Field row of the first column of the grid in the bottom half of the window.

Instead of dragging a field, you can choose a field from the Field drop-down list.

**4.** Click the Criteria row in the first column and type the criteria to limit the records you want to see.

For example, if you only want to see items that cost more that $10, put the Cost per Item field in the Field row of the first column, and type **>10** in the Criteria row.

***See also*** "Limiting Records with Criteria Expressions," in this part.

**5.** Repeat Steps 3 and 4 to add other fields and criteria to the grid.

**6.** (Optional) Choose a field by which to sort the resulting table.

Set a sort order by displaying the drop-down list for the Sort row in the column that contains the field you want to sort by — choose Ascending or Descending. This option tells Access to sort the table that results from the advanced filter in ascending or descending order, using the field listed in the same column as the sort key.

**7.** When you have created all the criteria that you need, click the Apply Filter button to see the resulting table.

Access displays all the fields in the original table, but it filters the records and displays only those that meet the criteria.

After you see the data produced by your advanced filter, you can do several things with the resulting table:

✦ **Save it:** If you want to save your advanced filter, you have to save it in Design view. After you apply the filter, return to Design view by choosing Record⇨Filter⇨Advanced Filter/Sort and click the

Save As Query button to save the advanced filter. You can get to the filter after it's saved through the Queries tab of the Database window.

✦ **Filter it:** Use the filter buttons and Record➪Filter to filter the table even more.

 ✦ **Print it:** Click the Print button.

✦ **Sort it:** The best way to sort is to use the Sort row in the design grid. But you can use the Sort Ascending or Sort Descending buttons to sort the query-result table by the field that the cursor is in.

✦ **Fix it:** Choose Record➪Filter➪Advanced Filter/Sort to display the Design view to fix the criteria or other information in the grid.

 ✦ **Add data to it:** Add data to the table by clicking the New Record button and typing the data.

✦ **Edit data:** Edit data the same way that you would in the datasheet and press F2.

✦ **Delete records:** You can delete entire records if you want — click the record you want to delete and click the Delete Record button.

✦ **Toggle between the filtered table and the full table:** Click the Apply Filter button. If you're looking at the full table, clicking the Apply Filter button displays the filtered table (according to the last filter that you applied). If you're looking at the filtered table, clicking the Apply Filter button displays the full table.

# Inserting Fields in a Query Grid

You can move a field from the table pane to the query grid in three easy ways:

✦ Double-click the field name. Access moves the field to the first open column in the grid.

✦ Drag the field name from the table pane to the field row of an unused column in the query grid.

✦ Use the drop-down list in the Field row of the query grid to choose the field you want. If you use this method with a multiple-table query, you may find it easier to choose the table name from the drop-down Table list before selecting the field name. If you don't have the Table row in your query grid, *see* "Displaying or Hiding Table Names," in this part.

You can put all the field names from one table into the query grid in two ways:

✦ **Put one field name in each column of the grid.** If you have criteria for all the fields, you can put one field name in each column of the query grid in just two steps. Double-click the table name where it appears in the table pane of the Design view to select all the fields in the table. Then drag the selected names to the grid. When you release the mouse button, Access puts one name in each column.

✦ **Put all the field names in one column.** This method is useful if you want to find something that could be in any field or if you have one criterion for all the fields in the table. The asterisk appears above the first field name in each Table window. Drag the asterisk to the grid to tell Access to include all field names in one column. The asterisk is also available as the first choice in the drop-down Field list — it appears as TableName.*.

# Limiting Records with Criteria Expressions

Criteria enable you to limit the data that the query displays. Although you can use a query to see data from related tables together in one record, the power of queries is that you can filter your data to see only records that meet certain criteria. You use the Criteria and Or rows in the query grid to tell Access exactly which records you want to see.

Access knows how to *query by example* (QBE). In fact, the grid in Design view is sometimes called the QBE grid. QBE makes creating criteria easy. If you tell Access what you're looking for, Access goes out and finds it. For example, if you want to find values equal to 10, the criteria is simply 10. Access then finds records that match that criteria.

The most common type of criteria are called logical expressions. A *logical expression* gives a yes or no answer. Access shows you the record if the answer is yes, but not if the answer is no. The operators commonly used in logical expressions include <, >, AND, OR, and NOT.

## Querying by example

If you want to find all the addresses that are in Virginia, the criterion for the state field is simply the following:

Virginia

You may want to add another criterion in the next line (OR) to take care of different spellings, as follows:

VA

Access puts the text in quotes for you. The result of the query is all records that have either *Virginia* or *VA* in the state field.

## Using operators in criteria expressions

The simplest way to use the query grid is to simply tell Access what you're looking for by typing a value you want to match in the Criteria row for the field. But often, your criteria are more complicated than "all records with Virginia in the state field." You use operators in your criteria expressions to tell Access about more complex criteria.

This table lists the operators that you're likely to use in a criteria expression:

| Relational Operator | What It Does |
| --- | --- |
| = | Finds values equal to text, a number, or date/time |
| < > | Finds values not equal to text, a number, or date/time |
| < | Finds values less than a given value |
| < = | Finds values less than or equal to a given value |
| > | Finds values greater than a given value |
| > = | Finds values greater than or equal to a given value |
| BETWEEN | Finds values between or equal to two values |
| IN | Finds values or text included in a list |
| LIKE | Finds matches to a pattern |

When you type your criteria, you don't have to tell Access that you're looking for Costs<10, for example. When you put <10 in the Criteria row, Access applies the criteria to the field that appears in the Field row of the same column. The following table shows some examples of criteria that use operators:

| Expressions with Operator | What the Operator Tells Access to Do |
| --- | --- |
| <10 | Finds record with values less than 10 |
| >10 | Finds records with values greater than 10 |
| <>10 | Finds records with values not equal to 10 |
| >10 AND <20 | Finds records with values between 10 and 20 |
| >=10 AND <=20 | Finds records with values between 10 and 20, including 10 and 20 |
| BETWEEN 10 AND 20 | The same as >=10 AND <=20 |
| IN ("Virginia", "VA") | Finds the values *Virginia* and *VA* |
| LIKE "A*" | Finds text beginning with the letter A. You can use LIKE with wildcards such as * to tell Access in general terms what you're looking for. For more information on the wildcards that Access recognizes, *see* "Limiting Data Entries with a Validation Rule," in Part III. |

## Using AND, OR, and NOT

The most common way to combine expressions that tell Access what you're looking for is to use AND, OR and NOT in your criteria. These three operators can be a little difficult to figure out, unless you aced Logic 101 in college. Here's exactly how they work:

| Simple Operator | How It Works in a Query |
|---|---|
| AND | Tells Access that a particular record must meet more than one criterion to be shown in the datasheet |
| OR | Tells Access that a particular record must meet only one of several criteria to be shown in the datasheet |
| NOT | Tells Access that a criterion has to be false for the record to be included in the datasheet |

You can combine operators in one criterion expression, such as when you are looking for the following:

```
>10 OR <18 NOT 15
```

This expression produces records with the values 11, 12, 13, 14, 16, and 17.

## Using multiple criteria

When you have criteria for only one field, you can use the OR operator in two different ways:

+ Type your expressions into the Criteria row separated by OR.

+ Type the first expression in the Criteria row, and type subsequent expressions using the Or rows in the query grid.

Whichever approach you take, the result is the same — Access displays records in the Datasheet that satisfy one or more of the Criteria expressions.

When you use criteria in different columns, Access assumes that you want to find records that meet all the criteria — in other words, that the criteria in each row are considered to be joined by AND statements. If you type criteria on the same row for two fields, a record has to meet both criteria to be displayed on the datasheet.

When you use the Or row, the expressions on each row are treated as though they are joined by AND, but the expressions on different rows are treated as though they are joined by OR. Access first looks at one row of criteria, and finds all the records that meet all the criteria on that row. Then it starts over with the next row of criteria, the Or row, and finds all the records that meet all the criteria on that row. A record only has to meet all the criteria on one row to be displayed in the datasheet.

For example, the following query produces a table including records of items that were either ordered from Lands' End and cost less than $50, or that were ordered from L. L. Bean and cost more than $50.

## Using dates, times, text, and values in criteria

Access does its best to recognize the types of data that you use in criteria and encloses elements of the expression between the appropriate characters. You are less likely to create criteria that Access doesn't understand, however, if you use those characters yourself.

The following table lists types of elements that you may include in a criteria expression and the character to use to make sure that Access knows that the element is text, a date, a time, a number, or a field name.

| Use This Type of Data . . . | In an Expression Like This . . . |
|---|---|
| Text | "text" |
| Date | #1-Feb-97# |
| Time | #12:00am# |
| Number | 10 |
| Field name | [field name] |

You can refer to dates or times by using any allowed format. December 25, 1996, 12/25/96, and 25-Dec-96 are all formats that Access recognizes. You can use AM/PM or 24-hour time.

# Saving a Query

You don't have to save a query. Often, queries are created on the fly to answer a question. There's no need to clutter your database with queries that you're unlikely to need again.

That said, you can certainly save a query when you need to. Use any of the following methods:

 ✦ In Design or Datasheet view, click the Save button or choose File⇨Save. If you haven't saved the query yet, Access asks you for a name for the query. Type the name and then click OK.

 ✦ Close the query (clicking the Close button is a popular method). If you've never saved the query, or if you've changed the query design since you last saved it, Access asks whether you want to save the query. If you've never saved the query, give it a name and then click OK; otherwise, click <u>Y</u>es to save the query.

TIP

I recommend giving your new query a name that tells you what the query does. That way, you won't have to open one query after another to find the one you're looking for.

# Sorting a Query

You can sort a table produced by a query in several ways. The first way is to use the Sort row in the query grid. Use the Sort row to tell Access which field to use to sort the datasheet.

To sort by a field, display your query in Design view and follow these steps:

*1.* Move the cursor to the Sort row in the column that contains the field according to which you want to sort.

*2.* Display the drop-down list for the Sort row.

Access displays the options for sorting: Ascending, Descending, and (not sorted).

*3.* Choose Ascending or Descending.

You can use the Sort row in the query grid to sort by more than one field. You may want to sort the records in the datasheet by last name, for example, but more than one person may have the same last name. You can specify another field (perhaps first name) as the second sort key. If you want, you can specify more than two fields by which to sort.

When you sort using more than one field, Access always works from left to right, first sorting the records by the first field (the primary sort key) that has Ascending or Descending in the Sort row, and then sorting any records with the same primary sort key value by the second sort key.

You can also sort the datasheet that results from the query, using the same technique that you use to sort any datasheet: Click the field that you want to sort by and then click the Sort Ascending or Sort Descending button. *See also* "Sorting Your Data," in Part III.

You cannot choose a field that is a Memo or OLE Data Type to sort by.

# Using a Query Wizard

If you click the New button in the Queries tab of the Database window, you see not one but four wizards to help you build your query. The wizard that you use depends on what you want your query to do.

The following table lists the four query wizards and tells when you may find each useful:

| Query Wizard | When to Use It |
|---|---|
| Simple Query Wizard | Use this wizard when you want to build a select query. If you want to perform summary calculations with the query, the wizard can help you. If you have criteria, however, you still have to enter them in Design view, so the Simple Query Wizard is not a huge improvement over designing the query yourself. *See also* "Creating a Select Query," in this part, for specifics about using the Simple Query Wizard. |
| Crosstab Query Wizard | Use this wizard when you want to create a crosstab query. *See also* "Creating a Crosstab Query," in this part, for specific information about using the Crosstab Query Wizard. |
| Find Duplicates Query Wizard | Use this wizard when you want to find duplicates in the database. |
| Find Unmatched Query Wizard | Use this wizard when you want to find records with no corresponding records in related tables. |

Wizards give you help creating queries, but the queries that they create are just like the ones you create — you can see them in Design or Datasheet view and do anything with them that you might do with any other query of the same type.

 Using a query wizard and studying the Design view of the queries that they create is a good way to learn how to use some of the more advanced features of queries.

Start a query wizard by following these steps:

*1.* Display the Queries tab of the Database window.

*2.* Click the New button.

Access displays the New Query dialog box.

*3.* Select the wizard that you want to use.

On the left side of the dialog box, Access displays a brief summary of what the wizard does.

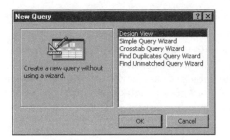

4. Click OK.

Access starts the wizard that you chose.

*See also* "Working with Wizards," in Part I.

## Find Duplicates Query Wizard

Use this wizard when you want to find duplicate entries in a field in a table or query. The Find Duplicates Query Wizard could help you find records with the same name and different addresses, for example.

The Find Duplicates Query Wizard needs to know the following things:

+ What table or query you want it to examine. The wizard displays table names first — if you want to see query names, click the Queries or Both radio button.

+ The fields in the table or query you picked that might have duplicate information that you're interested in. Select fields that might have duplicate entries and click the right arrow to move them into the Duplicate-value fields list box.

+ Any additional fields that you want to see in the datasheet produced by the query. Seeing additional fields can be useful if you're editing or deleting duplicated records.

+ The name of the query.

When you click the Finish button and display the datasheet, you see a list of records. Duplicates are listed in groups. You can edit this datasheet to update your data or to delete unneeded records.

## Find Unmatched Query Wizard

The Find Unmatched Query Wizard finds records in one table that have no matching records in another, related table. You may store orders in one table and details about customers in another table, for example. If the tables are linked by, say, a Customer Number field, the Unmatched Query Wizard could tell you whether you have any customers listed in the orders table who aren't listed in the customers table.

The Find Unmatched Query Wizard needs to know the following things:

✦ The table (or query) in which all records should have related records. In the example earlier in this section, this table is the table where the details of each order are stored. (You should have a related record about each customer.) If you want to choose a query, click the Queries or Both radio button.

✦ The name of the table that contains the related records. In the example, this table is the table where the details about each customer are stored. If you want to see queries in addition to tables, click the Queries or Both radio button.

✦ The names of the related fields. Access makes a guess, especially if there is a field in each table with the same name. (It's a little odd that Access can't figure out the names of the related fields by itself, especially if you've defined relationships, but there it is.)

✦ The fields that you want to see in the datasheet resulting from the query.

✦ The name for the query.

# Viewing Table Relationships in a Query

Although you can perform a query on unrelated tables, you're likely to get more useful results if the tables are linked. When you put unrelated tables in a query, Access attempts to find a relationship between the tables by comparing the fields in each table. If Access finds two fields that have the same name and the same type of data, it automatically creates a join between them.

***See also*** "Relating (Linking) Tables," in Part II, for more information about how to link tables.

You can view the Relationships window by right-clicking the table pane of the Query Design view and choosing Relationships from the shortcut menu. When you finish creating or editing relationships, close the Relationships window to return to Query Design view. The changes that you made in the Relationships window are reflected in the table pane.

If the relationship lines look all tangled in the Table pane of Query Design view, you can move the tables around, just as you can when you view relationships. Just click the title bar of the table and drag it to a new position.

# Viewing Top Values

 If all you care about is the top values produced by a query, you can tell Access so. Use the Top Values option in the toolbar in Query Design view to see the top records produced by the query. A value in the Top Values option shows you that many records in the datasheet; a percentage shows you that percentage of the records that the query found.

Here's what you do to display the top values found by a query:

**1.** Create your query with all the fields and criteria that you need.

**2.** Double-check the first sort field, which determines the records that end up at the top of the datasheet.

**3.** Change the Top Values option by typing a value or a value followed by a percent sign.

You can also choose a value from the drop-down list.

**4.** Click the View button to see only the top values in the datasheet.

# Working with Query Datasheets

The result of a query looks a great deal like a table — in fact, it really is a table that you can sort, filter, navigate and type data in. This subset of your data is sometimes called a *dynaset*. The word *dynaset* is used because the data that you see in the datasheet is a dynamic subset of your data.

A dynaset is dynamic because the result of a query is updated to reflect changes in the data in your tables. The actual records displayed in a dynaset — the result of a query — are not stored in the database; only the design of the query is stored, and each time you open the query in Datasheet view, it determines which records fit the query criteria.

Because working with queries in Datasheet view is similar to working with tables in Datasheet view, you should turn to Part III for specific instructions on working in the Datasheet view.

***See also*** "Editing Data in a Datasheet," in Part III.

***See also*** "Adding Data to Your Datasheet," in Part III.

***See also*** "Moving Around a Datasheet," in Part III.

***See also*** "Filtering Your Data," in Part III.

***See also*** "Sorting Your Data," in Part III.

***See also*** "Formatting Datasheets," in Part III.

 To return to Query Design view, click the View button.

# Part V

# Reporting Results

Compiling exactly the data you're looking for is all fine and good, but making that data look great so that you can print it, pass it around, and astound your friends is the whole point, right? In Access 97, spiffy output comes in the form of reports.

## In this part . . .

- ✔ Using the Report Wizard to create awesome reports
- ✔ Creating a report in Report Design view
- ✔ Creating AutoReports
- ✔ Formatting reports
- ✔ Creating sections in your reports to group your data
- ✔ Creating charts with the Chart Wizard
- ✔ Creating labels with the Label Wizard

# About Reports

Reports are the best way to take information from Access 97 and put it on paper. In a report, you can choose the size and format in which to display your data. You can even add pictures and graphs to your reports.

You can also use calculations in reports to create totals, subtotals, and other results. You can create invoices with reports, as well as other output that summarizes part of your database. Thanks to the trusty Label Wizard, reports are also the best way to create mailing labels from the data contained in a database.

You can create a report from one table or query, or from several linked tables and queries. You can even create a report from a filtered table.

## Adding Calculations to a Report

If you want to create a calculation in a report, you must first have somewhere to put the calculation. In reports, the place to put expressions is in a text box, so the first step in adding a calculation is to create a text box in your report.

**TIP**

Calculations often go in section and report footers, summarizing the data in that section or in the entire report.

To create a text box, follow these steps:

*1.* Display the report in Design view.

> **See also** "Previewing Your Report" and "Creating a Report Using Design View" later in this part.

**ab|** *2.* Click the Text Box button in the Toolbox.

*3.* Click and drag in the report design to create a box in the place where you want the calculation result to be displayed (and that is the right size to display the result of the expression).

> The box doesn't have to be big enough to display the whole expression that you're going to enter. It only needs to be large enough to display the result of the expression. As you type the expression, the display scrolls so that you can see the part of the expression that you're working on.

*4.* Click inside the box to display the cursor.

*5.* Type an equal sign (=) to begin the expression.

*6.* Type the expression that you want Access to calculate.

> **See also** "Calculating Fields (Building Expressions)," in Part IV.

If you want to use the Expression Builder to create an expression, you need to display the properties for the text box. Select the text box and then click the Properties button on the toolbar.

***See also*** "Selecting Parts of a Report," in this part.

The expression appears in the Control Source box on the Data tab. To use the Expression Builder, click the Control Source box and then click the Build button that appears to the right of the option.

You may find the Running Sum property useful. If you choose Yes for this option, Access creates a running sum — that is, it adds each section's total to the total calculated for the section(s) that appear before it in the report.

## Adding Color to a Report

The Formatting toolbar provides options for adding color to a report. You can change the color of text, backgrounds, and lines by using one of three buttons on the Formatting toolbar. The following table lists the three buttons on the toolbar that control color, what they're called, and how they work:

| Button | What It's Called | What It Does |
|---|---|---|
| | Fill/Back Color | Changes the color of the background of the selected object or the background of the selected section when no control is selected |
| | Font/Fore Color | Changes the color of the text in the selected object |
| | Line/Border Color | Changes the color of the border (the box around the object) of the selected object; also changes the color of a selected line |

You use the three buttons the same way. Follow these steps:

*1.* Select the object that you want to work with.

*2.* Click the arrow to the right of the button that changes colors.

Access displays a palette of colors.

*3.* Click the color that you want to use.

 If you want the object to be invisible or the same color as the general background, choose <u>T</u>ransparent from the top of the color grid.

# Adding Dates and Page Numbers

Access 97 is a whiz at many things, including dates and page numbers. Access can number the pages of your report or put today's date in a report — all you have to do is ask.

The most sensible place to add the date and page number is in the page header or page footer section of the report. The Report Wizard puts both the date and the page number (in the format Page X of Y) in the page footer for you.

## Inserting the date and/or time

If you want to add the date and/or time yourself, rather than relying on the Report Wizard, display the report in Design view and follow these steps:

*1.* Click the section (or *band*) in which you want the date or time to appear.

*2.* Choose Insert⇨Date and Time to insert the date, the time, or both. The Date and Time dialog box appears.

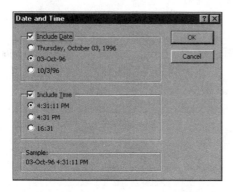

The Date and Time dialog box provides options for including the date, the time, or both, and allows you to choose the format.

*3.* Select Include Date and/or Include Time and then select the format you want. Check the Sample box to see how the date and/or time will appear on your report.

*4.* Click OK.

Access adds the date and/or time to the section of your report that you selected in Step 1.

TIP

You can move and format the date and time controls just as you do any other. *See also* "Moving an Object," "Changing Font and Font Size," and "Changing the Size of an Object," all in this part.

## *Inserting page numbers*

If you want to add page numbers yourself, rather than rely on the Report Wizard, display the report in Design view and follow these steps:

*1.* Choose Insert⇨Page Numbers. The Page Numbers dialog box appears.

> **Page Numbers**       ? ✕
>
> ┌─ Format ─────────────┐    ┌──── OK ────┐
> │ ○ Page N                    │    └────────────┘
> │ ◉ Page N of M           │    ┌──── Cancel ──┐
> └──────────────────────┘    └────────────┘
>
> ┌─ Position ───────────┐
> │ ○ Top of Page [Header] │
> │ ◉ Bottom of Page [Footer] │
> └──────────────────────┘
>
> Alignment:
> [ Center               ▼ ]
>
> ☑ Show Number on First Page

The Page Numbers dialog box gives you several choices about how your page numbers will appear on your report:

- **Format:** Select Page N to show only the current page number, or select Page N of M to show both the current page number and the total number of pages.

- **Position:** Decide whether the page numbers will appear in the page header or the page footer.

- **Alignment:** Click the down-arrow of this list box and choose Center (centers page numbers between the margins), Left (aligns page numbers with the left margin), Right (aligns page numbers with the right margin), Inside (prints page numbers alternately on the right and left sides of facing pages), or Outside (prints page numbers alternately on the left and right sides of facing pages).

- **Show Number on First Page:** Deselect (remove the check mark from) this option if you want to hide the page number on the first page of your report (a great way to keep your title page spiffy).

*2.* Change the options in the dialog box to suit your purposes.

*3.* Click OK.

Access puts the page number in the section you selected (Top of Page or Bottom of Page).

You can move and format the date and time controls just as you do any other. *See also* "Moving an Object," "Changing Font and Font Size," and "Changing the Size of an Object," all in this part.

# Aligning Report Objects

The three alignment buttons on the Formatting toolbar allow you to tell Access how to align the contents of a control.

To change the alignment of the contents of a control, follow these steps:

*1.* Select the object.

*2.* Click the appropriate alignment button: Align Left, Center, or Align Right.

Align Left

Align Right

Center

***See also*** "Moving an Object," for information on aligning controls (rather than the contents of the control).

# Changing Date or Number Formats

To change the format of a date or number in a field control, you need to use the Format property for the control. Follow these steps to display the properties for the control and change the format:

*1.* Select the control.

 *2.* Display the control's properties by clicking the Properties button.

*3.* Click the Format option (in the All and the Format tabs).

*4.* Choose the format that you want to use from the drop-down list.

*5.* Close the Properties box.

# Changing Font and Font Size

Changing the font and font size of text in a report is one of the easiest formatting tasks. Just follow these steps:

*1.* Select the object that contains the text you want to format.

*2.* Display the drop-down list of fonts in the Font option on the toolbar. Select the font to format the object.

**3.** Display the drop-down list of font sizes in the Font Size option on the toolbar. Select the font size to format the object.

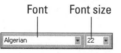

Font    Font size

You can make the text bold, italic, and/or underlined by clicking the Bold, Italic, and/or Underline button while the object is selected.

If you choose a font that makes the text to large to fit in the control, make the control larger. *See also* "Changing the Size of an Object," in this part.

# Changing Page Layout

Use the Page Setup dialog box to change the way Access prints your report on the page. Display the Page Setup dialog box by choosing File⇨Page Setup when working with the report in either Design view or Print Preview.

## Choosing landscape versus portrait

To choose whether the report should appear in *landscape* (longer than it is tall) or *portrait* (taller than it is long) orientation, follow these steps:

*1.* Display the Page Setup dialog box by choosing File⇨Page Setup.

*2.* Click the Page tab at the top of the dialog box.

*3.* Select the Portrait or Landscape radio button.

*4.* Close the dialog box.

## Adjusting margins

To change the margins for the report, follow these steps:

*1.* Display the Page Setup dialog box by choosing File⇨Page Setup.

*2.* Click the Margins tab at the top of the dialog box.

*3.* Change the Top, Bottom, Left, and Right margins as necessary.

*4.* Close the dialog box.

*See also* "Changing Margins," in Part VII.

## Printing in columns

If your report takes up less than half the width of a page, you can tell Access to print it in multiple columns. The options for columns are in the Page Setup dialog box.

To create columns in your report, follow these steps:

*1.* Display the Page Setup dialog box by choosing File➪Page Setup.

*2.* Click the Columns tab to view options for columns.

*3.* Use the Number of Columns setting to tell Access how many columns you want on each page.

*4.* Use the Column Layout settings to tell Access the order in which it should print on the page.

Access can work across a row before starting a new row (Across, Then Down) or work down a column before starting the next column (Down, Then Across).

*5.* Click OK to close the dialog box.

If you tell Access to use more columns than will fit on the page, you get an error message. Try using fewer columns, or try using landscape orientation (Orientation options appear on the Page tab of the Page Setup dialog box). If the columns fit, Access rearranges the print preview of the report; look at it and see whether you like what you've done.

You may want to use the other options in the Columns tab of the Page Setup dialog box, which are described in the following table:

| Option | What It Does |
|---|---|
| Row Spacing | Tells Access how much space (in inches) to leave between rows (A row is one record's worth of data.) |
| Column Spacing | Tells Access how much space (in inches) to leave between columns |
| Width | Specifies the width of the column (Access sets this option automatically; if you make the width smaller, the data may not fit in the column.) |
| Height | Specifies the height of a row (Access sets this option automatically.) |
| Same As Detail | Tells Access to size the column to fit the Detail section of the report when a check appears in the check box |

# Changing the Size of an Object

You can change the size of a control by clicking and dragging the border of the control while you're in Design view. Follow these steps:

*1.* Select the object whose size you want to change.

Anchors (little black boxes) appear around the selected object.

*See also* "Selecting Parts of a Report," in this part.

*2.* Move the mouse pointer to one of the anchors.

The pointer turns into a two-headed arrow, indicating that you can change the size of the box.

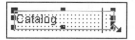

*3.* Drag the edge of the box so that the object is the size you want it to be.

The Format➪Size menu has additional options that allow you to change the size of an object:

✦ If you just want an object to be just the right size to display its contents, choose Format➪Size➪To Fit.

✦ If you want several objects to be the same size, select all the objects and then choose Format➪Size➪To Tallest, To Shortest, To Widest, or To Narrowest. Access makes all the objects the same size. If you choose To Shortest, for example, Access changes all the objects to the same size as the shortest object that was selected when you chose the menu option.

# Copying Formatting from One Control to Another

After you've gone to the effort of prettifying one control, why reinvent the wheel to make another control match it? You can simply copy the formatting from one control to another by using the Format Painter. The Format Painter copies all formatting — colors, fonts, font sizes, border sizes, border styles, and anything else that you can think of.

Follow these steps to copy formatting from one control to another.

*1.* Select the object that has the formatting you want to copy.

*2.* Click the Format Painter button on the toolbar. If you want to format more than one object, double-click the Format Painter button.

The Format Painter button now looks pushed in. When the mouse pointer is on an object that can be formatted, the pointer has a paintbrush attached to it. When the mouse pointer is on a part of the report that can't be formatted with the Format Painter, the paintbrush has a circle and line over it to indicate that you cannot format there.

*3.* Click the object to which you want to copy the formatting.

Access copies the formatting. If you used a single click to turn the Format Painter on, the mouse pointer loses its paintbrush. If you double-clicked to turn the Format Painter on, you can click additional objects to format them, too. To turn the Format Painter off, click the Format Painter button.

# Creating a New Report

The best way to create any report is to start with the Report Wizard, especially if you want to create a report that groups data using one or more fields. Chances are, the Report Wizard knows more about designing multilevel reports than you do, and when the Wizard finishes, you can take over and add distinctive formatting touches in Design view.

*See also* "Creating a Report with the Report Wizard," in this part.

*See also* "Creating a Report Using Design View," in this part.

*See also* "Creating Sections in a Report," in this part.

You create a report the same way that you create other objects in your database. Follow these steps:

*1.* Click the Database Window button.

*2.* Click the Reports tab.

*3.* Click the <u>N</u>ew button.

Access displays the New Report dialog box, giving you many choices for creating a new report.

If you're going to create a report in Design view, you can make your life easier by you selecting a table or query to base the report on. If you want to create a report that uses fields from more than one table, create a query that includes the fields you want to use in the report.

The following table describes the choices on the New Report dialog box and tells you when to use each of them.

| *Option in New Report Dialog Box* | *When to Use It* |
|---|---|
| Design View | When you want to design your own report from scratch in Report Design view. *See also* "Creating a Report Using Design View," in this part. |
| Report Wizard | When you want Access to create a report, using the fields, grouping, and sorting that you give it. *See also* "Creating a Report with the Report Wizard," in this part. |
| AutoReport: Columnar | When you want to create a report from one table or query and arrange data from each record on a separate page, with field names in a column on the left and the data for the field in a column on the right. *See also* "Creating a Report Using an AutoReport," in this part. |

*(continued)*

| Option in New Report Dialog Box | When to Use It |
| --- | --- |
| AutoReport: Tabular | When you want to create a report from one table or query and arrange the data in a table, with field names at the top of columns and data from each record displayed as a row in the table (as in a datasheet). *See also* "Creating a Report Using an AutoReport," in this part. |
| Chart Wizard | When you want to create a chart from data stored in one table or query. *See also* "Creating Charts with the Chart Wizard," in this part. |
| Label Wizard | When you want to put data from one table or query on labels. *See also* "Creating Labels with the Label Wizard," in this part. |

# Creating a Report from a Filtered Table

You can filter a table or record and create a report from the resulting records. When the data resulting from the filter changes, the report changes to match.

Here's how to do it:

*1.* Filter the table and display the filtered records in Datasheet view.

*2.* Click the arrow to the right of the New Object button and then choose AutoReport or Report from the drop-down list.

If you choose AutoReport, Access immediately displays a columnar AutoReport.

If you choose Report, Access displays the New Report dialog box.

*3.* Pick the method that you want to use to create the report, and design the report or have a wizard design it for you.

The filter that you used is transferred to the report. Changing the filter on the table that you used initially has no effect on the report.

# Creating a Report Using an AutoReport

AutoReports are an easy way to create a report out of one table or query. AutoReports don't have the flexibility that regular reports have — you can't create groups with an AutoReport, for example — but they are an excellent way to get your data into a report quickly. You can customize an AutoReport by using the formatting tricks described elsewhere in this part. *See also* "Formatting Reports with AutoFormat" and "Changing Font and Font Size," both in this part.

Access has two kinds of AutoReports: columnar and tabular. A tabular AutoReport looks like a datasheet. A columnar AutoReport prints one record per page, with the field names in a column on the left and the data for the record in a column on the right.

To create an columnar AutoReport, follow these steps:

> **1.** In the Database window, select the table or query that contains the data you want to display in a report.

> **2.** Click the arrow next to the New Object button and choose AutoReport from the drop-down list.
>
> Access creates the report.

Another way to create an AutoReport — and the only way to create a tabular AutoReport — is to click the New button in the Reports tab of the Database window. Access displays the New Report dialog box — choose the type of AutoReport and the table or query that you want it to use; then click OK. Access creates the report.

## Creating a Report Using Design View

You may have a personal thing against wizards, or you may just need to know how to make changes to a report yourself. Whichever is the case, this section covers how to add objects (also called *controls*) to your report.

Controls tell Access what you want to see on your report. Text, the contents of a field, and lines are all added to reports by using controls. I tell you how to add specific controls to your report later in this section. Follow these general steps to create the report itself:

> **1.** Display the Reports tab of the Database window.
>
> **2.** Click the New button.
>
> Access displays the New Report dialog box.
>
> **3.** From the list at the bottom of the dialog box, select the query or table on which you want to base the report.
>
> If you want to bind the report to more than one table, the easiest way is to create a query that includes all the fields you want to display in the report.

Binding a report to a query can be very useful — it means that you can create criteria for choosing the records that appear in your report so that Access doesn't include them all. You may want to make a report that includes only clients whose payments are overdue, for example, or you may want a report that includes only the addresses of people whom you're inviting to your wedding.

**4.** Choose the method that you want to use to create your report, Design view.

**5.** Click OK.

Access displays the Report Design view.

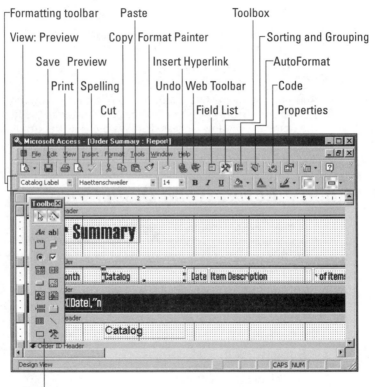

Formatting toolbar    Paste      Toolbox

View: Preview    Copy | Format Painter    Sorting and Grouping

Save   Preview      Insert Hyperlink    AutoFormat

Print | Spelling      Undo | Web Toolbar    Code

Cut      Field List    Properties

Toolbox

**6.** Save the report design by clicking the Save button on the toolbar.

Remember to save your report design often.

**7.** To see what your report will look like on paper, click the Print Preview or the View button.

***See also*** "Adding Calculations to a Report," "Creating Sections in a Report," "Changing Page Layout," and "Changing Font and Font Size," in this part for more information on how to make your report look the way you want it to.

For an in-depth discussion on how to design reports so that they do what you want them to do, see Chapters 18–20 of *Access 97 For Windows For Dummies,* or Chapters 21–23 of *Access For Windows 95 Bible* (both published by IDG Books Worldwide, Inc.).

To display the properties of any control, select the control and click the Properties button.

## Using tools in Report Design view

Creating reports is complicated enough that Access gives you a group of new tools to work with: the buttons and boxes in the Formatting toolbar and in the toolbox. Access also displays the grid in the background (to help you align objects in the report), as well as the rulers at the top and left of the design window.

You can choose which of these tools you want to appear by using the View menu when you're in Design view. Items with a check mark appear in the design window (except the Toolbox, which displays a highlighted icon instead of a check mark when the Toolbox is active).

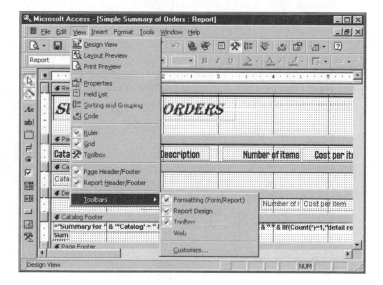

You can also display and close the Toolbox by clicking the Toolbox button on the toolbar. When the Toolbox is active, it appears only when Report Design view is the active window.

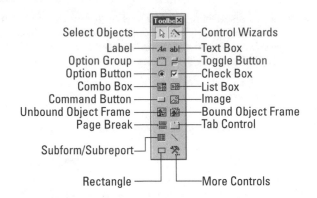

Select Objects — Control Wizards
Label — Text Box
Option Group — Toggle Button
Option Button — Check Box
Combo Box — List Box
Command Button — Image
Unbound Object Frame — Bound Object Frame
Page Break — Tab Control

Subform/Subreport

Rectangle — More Controls

Each type of object that you may want to add to your report has a different button in the toolbox — choose the type of object that you want and then click the spot in the report where you want to put the object.

You can move the Toolbox so that it appears along one edge of the Access window instead of floating free. To anchor the Toolbox to an edge, click on its title bar and drag the Toolbox to one edge of the screen. A gray outline shows you where the Toolbox will be when you drop it. When the gray outline appears in one row or column against one side of the Access window, release the mouse button. You can make the Toolbox free-floating again by clicking and dragging by the top (if the Toolbox is vertical) or the left of the bar. (In fact, you can perform this trick with any toolbar.)

## Adding a field

A report is made up of controls that tell Access what to display on the report. To display the contents of a field in a report, you have to create a control and tell Access to display the contents of a field in that control. The people who developed Access knew you would want to add fields to reports frequently. So they made it possible to add a field to a report with a single drag-and-drop procedure, rather than forcing you to use two steps — first creating the control and then telling Access to display the contents of a field in the control.

To add a control that displays the contents of a field to a report, display the report in Design view and follow these steps:

*1.* Display the Field List window by clicking the Field List button on the toolbar.

Access displays a small window that contains the names of the fields available to use on the report.

If you didn't bind a table or query to the report in the New Report dialog box, you won't have any fields to view. *See* "Creating a Report Using Design View" in this part.

**2.** Drag the field that you want to use in your report from the field list window to the report design. Drop the field in the place in the report design where you want the contents of the field to appear.

Access puts a field control and a label control in the report. The label control contains the name of the field, followed by a colon. The field control tells Access to display the contents of the field. You can edit or delete either control. ***See also*** "Editing Objects in a Report," later in this part.

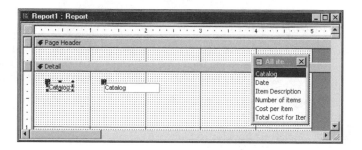

 You can put several fields in the report by Ctrl+clicking to select multiple field names. You can also select consecutive fields by clicking the first field and then Shift+clicking the last field that you want to select.

 If you want to get rid of the label that Access adds automatically or move the label to a different place in the report, select the label and then press Ctrl+X. To display the label in a different position, click the report design where you want the label to appear and then press Ctrl+V.

***See also*** "Selecting Parts of a Report," later in this part.

## Adding a line

 Remember that what you see in Report Design view is not exactly how the printed report will appear. Not everything you see in Design view is printed — for example, those little dots and the vertical lines you see in the background of the design view, as well as the boxes around the objects you've put in the report design, are all non-printing elements of the design. To see what the the printed report will look like, click the View button or the Print Preview button.

You can put a vertical, horizontal, or diagonal line into a report by adding it to the report design. If you want to create a box to surround an object, you actually want to work with the object's border. ***See also*** "Playing with Borders," later in this part.

Insert a line into a report by clicking the Line button in the Toolbox. Then move the mouse pointer into the report design, click where you want the line to begin, and drag to where you want the line to end. A line must begin and end within one section of the report design.

After you create a line, you can change its color and width by using the Line/Border Color and Line/Border Width buttons in the Formatting toolbar. You can delete the line by selecting it and pressing Del. You can move the line by clicking it and dragging it to a new position or by using the Cut and Paste buttons on the toolbar.

## Adding a label

If you want to create a text label that isn't attached to a field control, you can do so by using the Label button in the toolbox. For instance, you may want to create a label to display the name of the report.

Display the report in Design view and follow these steps to add a label to the report:

*1.* Click the Label button in the toolbox.

*2.* Click and drag in the report design to create a box the right size and position for your label.

*3.* Type the text that you want to appear in the label.

*4.* Press Enter.

**TIP**

If you want more than one line of text in your label box, press Ctrl+Enter to start a new line.

To edit the label, click the text box once to select it; then press F2 to edit the label. Press Enter when the edits are complete, or Esc to cancel the edits you have made.

## Adding pictures and other objects

You can add a picture to a report in several ways; the method that you use depends on how you want to use the picture. A picture can be bound or unbound (in fact, any object on the report can be bound or unbound). An *unbound* object is always the same, such as a logo. A *bound* object can change for different records. You may store a picture of each person in your address database, for example, and display the appropriate pictures next to the addresses in your report using a bound object.

You can link or insert a picture. A *linked* picture is stored in its own file; Access goes out and finds it when necessary. An *inserted* picture is stored in the Access database.

You can display a picture as an object in the report, or you can display it in the background of the report, like a watermark. If the picture is an object in the report, you can edit the picture by double-clicking it.

The easiest way to insert a picture into a report is to follow these steps:

*1.* Display the report in Design view.

*2.* Click the Insert Picture button in the toolbox.

*3.* Click the report where you want the picture to appear.

Access displays the Insert Picture dialog box, where you can find the file that contains the picture you want to display on the report.

*4.* In the Insert Picture dialog box, navigate your folders until you find the file that you need.

*5.* Select the file and then click OK.

You can even search the Web for an appropriate picture; just click the Search the Web button in the Insert Picture dialog box to launch Internet Explorer.

To find out more about using Internet Explorer to search the Web, see *Internet Explorer 3 For Windows For Dummies,* by Doug Lowe (published by IDG Books Worldwide, Inc.).

You can change the size and position of a picture the same way that you change the size or position of any object in the report. *See also* "Moving an Object" and "Changing the Size of an Object," both in this part.

To link to a picture, follow these steps:

*1.* Insert the picture.

*2.* Select the picture object.

*3.* Display the properties of the image by clicking the Properties button on the toolbar.

*4.* Change the Picture Type to Linked (use the drop-down list to see the options).

The Picture Type option is in the All tab of the Image dialog box.

You can delete a picture from the report by selecting it and pressing Del.

# Creating a Report with the Report Wizard

Using the Report Wizard is the best way to create a report. You may be happy with the resulting report, or you may want to edit the report further, but after you use the Report Wizard, you have a report to work with.

When you use the Report Wizard you don't have to gather all the data you want in the report into one table or query — the Report Wizard allows you to choose fields for the report from more than one table or query.

***See also*** "Working with Wizards," in Part I.

Here's how to use the Report Wizard:

***1.*** Display the New Report dialog box by displaying the Reports tab of the Database window and clicking the <u>N</u>ew button or by choosing <u>R</u>eport from the New Object button drop-down list.

***2.*** Select Report Wizard and then click OK.

Access displays the first Report Wizard window, where you select the fields that you want to use in your report.

```
┌─────────────────────────────────────────────────────────────┐
│ Report Wizard                                                │
│                                                              │
│  ┌──────────┐          Which fields do you want on your      │
│  │ ▦▦▦ → ▦  │          report?                               │
│  └──────────┘          You can choose from more than one     │
│                        table or query.                       │
│                                                              │
│  Tables/Queries:                                             │
│  ┌───────────────────────────┐                               │
│  │ Table: Catalogs         ▼ │                               │
│  └───────────────────────────┘                               │
│  Available Fields:           Selected Fields:                │
│  ┌──────────────────┐ ┌──┐  ┌──────────────────┐             │
│  │ Catalog        ▲ │ │ >│  │                  │             │
│  │ OrderPhone #   │ │ └──┘  │                  │             │
│  │ CustServicePhone #│ ┌──┐  │                  │             │
│  │ Fax #          │ │ │>>│  │                  │             │
│  │ Address1       │ │ └──┘  │                  │             │
│  │ Address2       │ │ ┌──┐  │                  │             │
│  │ City           │ │ │< │  │                  │             │
│  │ State        ▼ │ │ └──┘  │                  │             │
│  └──────────────────┘ ┌──┐  └──────────────────┘             │
│                       │<<│                                   │
│                       └──┘                                   │
│                                                              │
│        ┌────────┐  ┌──────┐ ┌──────┐  ┌────────┐             │
│        │ Cancel │  │<Back │ │Next >│  │ Finish │             │
│        └────────┘  └──────┘ └──────┘  └────────┘             │
└─────────────────────────────────────────────────────────────┘
```

***3.*** From the <u>T</u>ables/Queries list, select the first table or query from which you want to select fields.

***4.*** Add the fields that you want displayed in the report to the <u>S</u>elected Fields list.

***5.*** Repeat Steps 3 and 4 for fields in other tables or queries until all the fields that you want to display in the report appear in the <u>S</u>elected Fields list.

**6.** Click the <u>N</u>ext button to see the next window of the wizard.

The Report Wizard may display this window, which allows you to choose which table you want to use to group your data.

Double-click a table name to group the data in the report by using that table; then click <u>N</u>ext to continue to the next window, which lets you group fields.

**7.** Tell the Report Wizard how to group the fields.

In the example, I want to group my orders by catalog and date, followed by the information on which items were ordered on that date. Access also uses the fields that you group by to sort your data. You don't have to group your data if you don't want to — you can skip this window and go on to the next.

Select a field to group by double-clicking the field or by selecting it and then clicking the right-arrow button.

You can create a hierarchy of fields to group by double-clicking additional field names. You can change the importance of a field in the grouping hierarchy by selecting the field on the right side of the window and then clicking the up- and down-arrow buttons that are labeled Priority.

Click the Grouping Options button to display the Grouping Intervals dialog box, where you can specify exactly how to group records using the fields you chose as grouping fields.

The Grouping Intervals dialog box lets you select grouping intervals for each field — different data types have different grouping-interval options:

✦ If you are grouping by a field that contains a date, Access lets you group dates by day, month, year, and so on.

✦ If you are grouping by a field that contains numbers, Access lets you group values in 10s, 50s, 100s, 500s, 1,000s, 5,000s, and 10,000s so that you can categorize values by magnitude.

✦ If you are grouping by a field that contains text, Access allows you to group by using up to five initial letters.

✦ For all types of data, the Normal option groups by using the entire field. (Only records that have exactly the same value are grouped together.)

Click OK to leave the Grouping Intervals dialog box.

*8.* When you finish grouping your data, click the Next button to see options for sorting and summarizing.

Access sorts the report according to the first field by which you've specified that data be grouped. This window allows you to tell Access how you want to sort the detail section of the report. You don't have to change anything in this window if you don't need the detail section sorted in any particular order.

If you want to specify a sort order for the detail objects, display the drop-down list of field names next to the box labeled 1. Click the Sort button to change the sort order from ascending (A to Z) to descending (Z to A). Click the button again to change the sort order back to ascending. You can sort by up to four fields — use the additional boxes to specify additional fields on which to sort.

*9.* When you finish deciding how to sort the detail section of your report, you can click the Summary Options button to tell Access to display totals or other calculated summary data in the report.

Access displays the Summary Options dialog box.

The options displayed in the Summary Options dialog box depend on the data that you're displaying in your report.

**10.** Click check boxes to indicate the field that you want to summarize and what kind of calculation you want for the summary.

This dialog box also has options that allow you to show the Summary Only or the Detail and Summary data. If you choose Summary Only, the report displays only the result of the calculation, not the data from the records that were used to calculate the result. If you want to see the data in individual records, choose Detail and Summary data. This dialog box also has a check box to tell Access to Calculate percent of Total for Sums; Access then calculates the percentage of the total that each group represents.

**11.** When you're done with the Summary Options dialog box, click OK; you see the window with sorting options again. Then click Next in the Report Wizard window to view the next window.

Access displays the window that allows you to specify how to lay out your report.

**12.** Choose the layout that you prefer and the orientation that works best with your report.

You can preview the layout options by clicking one of the Layout radio buttons. The example box on the left changes to show you what the layout that you've chosen looks like.

**13.** Click Next to see the next window, where you choose the style that you prefer.

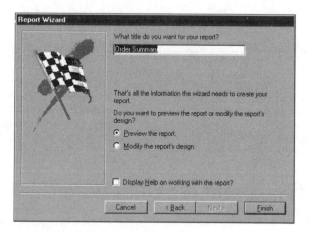

Styles consist of background shadings, fonts, font sizes, and the other formatting used for your report.

**14.** Select a style.

You can preview each style by clicking it.

**15.** Click the Next button to view the last window of the wizard.

**16.** Type a new name for the report (if you don't like the name that the Report Wizard has chosen).

If you want to view the report in Design view, click Modify the Report's Design; otherwise, the Preview the report radio button will be selected, and Access will show you the report in Print Preview. You can also tell Access that you want to see the Help window (which gives you hints on how to customize the report) by clicking the check box titled Display <u>H</u>elp on Working with the Report?

**17.** Click the <u>F</u>inish button to view your report.

Your computer may whir and grind for a minute before your report appears.

Although the Report Wizard does well setting up groups, it doesn't create a perfect report. Some controls may be the wrong size, and the explanatory text the wizard uses for calculated fields is a little academic. Display the report in Design view to fix anything that's wrong with it. *See also* "Changing the Size of an Object," "Editing Objects in a Report," and "Moving an Object," all in this part.

# Creating Charts with the Chart Wizard

If you want to create charts in Access, the Chart Wizard is a good way to get started. To use the Chart Wizard, you must have installed the Advanced Wizards. You may need to dig out your CD-ROM or floppy disks to install these wizards because they are not installed during the standard installation.

*See also* "Working with Wizards," in Part I.

Here's how to use the Chart Wizard to create a graph:

*1.* Display the Reports tab of the Database window and click the New button.

Access displays the New Report dialog box.

*2.* Select Chart Wizard, choose the table or query that contains the data you want to chart, and then click the OK button.

Access displays the first window of the wizard, where you choose the fields you want to chart.

*3.* Select the fields that you want to chart by double-clicking them.

The fields you chose move into the Fields for Chart box. If you want to chart values by date, make sure that you include the field that contains the date value. For example, if you want to chart calls per week for each week of the year, you need to choose both the field that contains the number of calls data and the field that contains the information about when the calls were received.

*4.* Click Next to see the next window.

*5.* Select the type of chart that you want to create.

When you select a chart type, the wizard gives you some information about the chart type and the kind of data that makes an effective chart of that type.

*6.* Click Next when you've chosen the chart type that you want to use.

The next window is tricky — it's where you tell the wizard how you want the chart to appear.

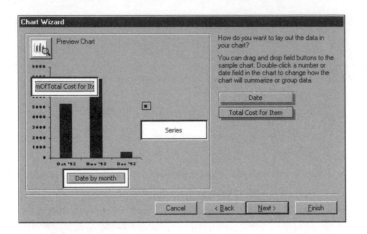

The chart shows three labels: the X-axis (horizontal) label (Date by Month), the Y-axis (vertical) label (SumOfTotal Cost for Items), and the series that are displayed in the chart (which will appear as a legend in the chart).

Double-click a box on the left side of the window to see more detail. When you double-click Date by Month, for example, you see a dialog box that allows you to change the grouping shown in the chart to years, quarters, days, and so on. If you double-click SumOfTotal Cost for Items, you see a dialog box that allows you to change the calculation from sum to one of the other aggregate functions.

The fields that you've chosen are buttons on the right side of the window; drag them to the chart on the left side to use them as labels and to tell Access how to build the chart. If Access used the wrong fields in any of the labels, you can drag the field name from the left side of the chart to the right side.

**7.** When you finish, click Next to see the next window.

**8.** Give the chart a name, tell Access whether you want to see a legend in the chart (the part of the chart that labels the fields used), and specify whether you want to see the chart in Print Preview or Design view.

**9.** Click Finish to see what you've created.

# Creating Labels with the Label Wizard

If you need to print your data on labels, the Label Wizard is a great way to get what you need in the right format.

Before you launch the Label Wizard, you need to gather data for the labels together in one table or query. You may also want to have your labels on hand, unless you know by heart the Avery number or the exact dimensions.

After you get your data together in one table or query and determine the size or Avery number of your labels, you're ready to run the Label Wizard and let it make your labels.

***See also*** "Working with Wizards," in Part I.

Follow these steps to let the Label Wizard help you make labels:

**1.** Display the New Report dialog box by clicking the <u>N</u>ew button in the Reports tab of the Database window.

**2.** Select Label Wizard, and choose the table or query that contains the data for the labels; then click OK to start the wizard.

Access displays the window where you tell it about the labels that you're using.

**3.** If you're using Avery labels, make sure that the Show custom label sizes check box does not have a check mark in it (click the check box to remove the check mark, if you need to). Use the Unit of Measure and Label Type radio buttons to display the appropriate list of Avery labels and then select the Avery label you'll be using.

If you're using non-Avery labels, click the Show custom label sizes check box and select the label size you need, if it is displayed. If you need to create a new label definition, click the Customize button to open the New Label Size dialog box. If no custom labels are defined, you can create a new label definition by clicking the <u>N</u>ew button. Access displays the New Label dialog box for you to type a name and select a unit of measure, label type, and orientation. Next, define the labels by filling in the measurements on the sample label page at the bottom of the dialog box. You need to know the dimensions of the labels and the distance between labels. You also need to specify margins on the labels — that is, the distance between the edge of each label and the data on the label.

If any custom label definitions already exist, select a label definition similar to the labels you're using. Then click the Duplicate button to make a copy of the label definition and display the Edit Label dialog box. Edit the label name and definition. This approach is easier than starting from scratch!

After you've defined the label, click OK on the New Label Size or the Edit Label dialog box, and then click the Close button on the New Label Size dialog box to return to the first window of the wizard.

Select the custom label definition that you just created.

**4.** Click the <u>N</u>ext button to see the next window of the wizard.

Access displays the next wizard window, where you specify the Font name, Font size, Font weight, and Text color for the labels. You can also choose to make the text Italic or Underlined.

**5.** Choose formatting for the label.

The format that you choose applies to the entire label; you can't format each field separately.

**6.** Click the <u>N</u>ext button.

Access displays the next window of the wizard, where you specify which fields you want to appear on the label.

**7.** Specify the fields that you want to use in the label.

Put a field in the Prototype Label box by double-clicking it (or by selecting it and then clicking the right-arrow button). Unlike the other wizards that you've used, this wizard does not require each field to appear on a separate line; the fields should appear in the Prototype Label list box the same way that you want them to appear in the label.

Press Enter or ↓ to move to a new row in the Prototype Label box; otherwise, all the field names will be in the same line. You can add punctuation or additional characters by typing them.

If you are creating address labels, for example, the Prototype label window may end up looking like the one shown in the following figure.

**Label Wizard**

What would you like on your mailing label?

Construct your label on the right by choosing fields from the left. You may also type text that you would like to see on every label right onto the prototype.

Available fields:

Fax #
Address1
Address2
City
State
Zip
E-mail

Prototype label:

{Catalog}
{Address1}
{Address2}
{City}, {State} {Zip}

[ Cancel ]  [ < Back ]  [ Next > ]  [ Finish ]

**8.** Click the <u>N</u>ext button to see the next window, which allows you to choose fields on which to sort.

**9.** Select the field by which you want Access to sort the labels.

Choose the field in the usual way — by double-clicking it or by selecting it and then clicking the right-arrow button. You can select additional fields on which to sort, if you want to.

**10.** Click <u>N</u>ext to see the final window of the wizard.

**11.** Give the report a name (or accept the one that Access suggests).

**12.** Choose either See the labels as they will look printed (which displays the report in Print Preview) or Modify the label design (which displays the report Design view) by selecting one of the radio buttons.

You may also want to use the Display Help on working with labels check box to display a Help window as well as the Design view or Print Preview of your labels.

**13.** Click <u>F</u>inish to tell the Label Wizard to make your labels.

After you close the wizard, you have to make any additional changes in Report Design view.

# Creating Sections in a Report

In Design view, your report is broken into parts, which are called *sections* or *bands*. Sections come in pairs around the Detail section of the report, which is the meat of the report sandwich.

Adding additional sections to a report allows you to group data using a particular field — if you have a number of records with the same value in a field, you can display those records together on the report. For example, if you have a file that stores the date of a transaction, you can create a Date section and then group records that have the same date.

For more information about grouping data in reports, see Chapter 18 of *Access 97 For Windows For Dummies*, by John Kaufeld. If you're *really* into the heavy-duty details of creating reports, check out Chapter 21 of *Access For Windows 95 Bible,* by Cary Prague and Michael Irwin. (Both books are, of course, published by IDG Books Worldwide, Inc.)

The following table lists the different sections that a report can display and how to use each section:

| Report Section | Where It Appears and How It's Used |
| --- | --- |
| Report Header and Footer | Appears at the beginning and end of the report. This section is where you put summary information about the entire report. The report header usually consists of a title, a date, or other information that is pertinent to the entire report. The report footer may contain summary calculations for the entire report, such as a grand total. |
| Page Header and Footer | Appears at the top and bottom of each page. The page header and footer may include information such as the name of the report, the date, and the page number. |
| Section Header and Footer | Appears at the top and bottom of each grouping and may include data about the particular grouping. Your report may have more than one section and footer — one for each grouping of your data in the report. The section footer may include a subtotal. |
| Detail | Appears after each section header, or after the report header, if your report has no additional sections. Displays values for each record. The detail section may be repeated many times in a printed report, if the data is grouped. For instance, if your report is grouped by date, the detail section displays information for each date group. The detail section may contain calculated fields — for instance, you can create an expression that calculates the total cost for an item (the item cost × the number of items ordered). |

In Report Design view, each section has a specific place. The gray bar names the section, and the items appearing underneath the bar appear each time that section of the report prints.

The report header and footer each print only once, but the page header and footer appear at the top and bottom of each printed page, and the section header and footer and the detail section can appear many times in the report, depending on how the data is grouped.

```
Simple Summary of Orders : Report                                    _ □ ×
      · · · · 1 · · · | · · · 2 · · · | · · · 3 · · · | · · · 4 · · · | · · · 5 · · · | · · · 6 · · · | · · · 7
  ✦ Report Header

  Summary of Orders

  ✦ Page Header
                                Item Description    Number of items  Cost per item  Total Cost for Item
  ✦ Catalog Header
  Catalog            Date
  ✦ Detail
                          Item Description       Number of Cost per item      Total Cost
  ✦ Catalog Footer
  Total Cost for Order                                                  =Sum([To
  ✦ Page Footer

  =Now()                                                  ="Page " & [Page] & " of " & [Pages]
  ✦ Report Footer
  Grand Total                                                          =Sum([Total C
```

## Creating a new section

Before you start creating new sections, you need to have a good understanding of how sections work. Use the Report Wizard to get started with your report and then use the skills discussed in this section to fine-tune your report. ***See also*** "Creating a Report with the Report Wizard," earlier in this part.

When you create a new report in Design view, you get a three-section report with the Page Header, Detail, and Page Footer sections. If you want to add or delete sections, read on. (You can't delete the Detail section, by the way — you'd end up with nothing in your report.)

When you create a new section in a report, you are changing the way the detail section of the report is grouped. You can't just create a new section before you decide what you'll use the section for — each section is controlled by a field, which is then used to group the detail section.

To create new sections in your report, display the report in Design view and then click the Sorting and Grouping button on the toolbar (or choose <u>V</u>iew⇨<u>S</u>orting and Grouping) to display the Sorting and Grouping dialog box. The following steps lead you through the specifics:

*1.* Click the Sorting and Grouping button on the toolbar.

Access displays the Sorting and Grouping dialog box, which displays any fields that are currently being used for sorting or grouping your report.

**2.** To add a section, move your cursor to a blank row and select a field from the Field/Expression drop-down list.

**3.** Access automatically uses ascending sort order for the new field; if you want to sort in descending order, choose Descending from the Sort Order drop-down list.

**4.** To make the field a group header, use the Group Properties settings at the bottom of the dialog box.

Choose Yes from the Group Header drop-down list. Access adds the grouping symbol to the field in the top part of the dialog box. You may also want to turn the Group Footer on, if you want the section to have a footer.

**5.** Close the Sorting and Grouping dialog box. Access adds the new section to the report design.

**6.** Click the Save button to save changes to the report design.

The preceding steps are sufficient to create a new group. The other Group Properties fine-tune the way that the group works. The following table lists the settings in the Group Properties section of the Sorting and Grouping dialog box and what each does.

| Group Property | What It Does |
| --- | --- |
| Group Header | Allows you to choose whether you want the report to contain a header section for this group. Choose Yes or No from the drop-down list. |
| Group Footer | Allows you to choose whether you want the report to contain a footer section for this group. Choose Yes or No from the drop-down list. |
| Group On | Allows you to choose the size of the group. If the field you're using to group by contains dates, for example, you can group by each value or by day, week, month, year, and so on. |

| Group Interval | Allows you to choose the size of the interval from the drop-down list. You must have chosen an option other than Each Value from the Group On list. |
| --- | --- |
| Keep Together | Allows you to choose whether the group should appear all on one page, or whether the section can be split and printed on more than one page. Select No to split the section over two pages. Select Whole Group if you want the section to always appear on one page. Select With First Detail if you want the group header to always appear on the same page with at least one detail record. |

## Deleting a section

Be aware that when you delete a section, you also delete all the controls (that is, all the objects) in the field.

To remove a section, display the report in Design view and follow these steps:

1. Click the Sorting and Grouping button on the toolbar.

   Access displays the Sorting and Grouping dialog box, with the names of fields used for sorting and grouping. Fields used for grouping appear with the grouping icon to their left.

2. Select the row for the group that you want to delete.

   The easiest way is to click that little grouping icon.

3. Press the Del key.

   Access asks whether you're sure that you want to delete the group and all the controls in the group.

4. If you're sure, click <u>Y</u>es.

5. Close the Sorting and Grouping dialog box.

## Adding and deleting report headers and footers

If you want to add a report header and a report footer to your report, all you need to do is display the report in Design view and then choose <u>V</u>iew⇨Report <u>H</u>eader/Footer. When the Report header and footer appear, a check mark appears beside the Report <u>H</u>eader/ Footer option on the menu.

To get rid of the report header and footer, choose <u>V</u>iew⇨Report <u>H</u>eader/Footer again to turn the check mark off.

If you want to display only a report header, change the height of the header by clicking and dragging the bottom border of the header up to the top border of the header. Perform the same actions with a report footer to delete a footer from your report.

## Adding and deleting page headers and footers

If you want to add a or delete the page header and page footer, display the report in Design view and choose View➪Page Header/Footer.

If you want just a page header or just a footer, change the height of the section that you don't want to use to zero by clicking and dragging the bottom border of the section up to the top border of the section.

You can tell Access not to print the page header and footer on the first and last pages of the report. Why would you want to do so, you ask? Because the page header and footer sometimes repeat information that's already included in the report header and footer (which appear on the first and last pages), so having both on the same page may be redundant.

You can specify which pages the page header and footer print on using the Report Properties dialog box. Display this dialog box by double-clicking the report selector (the gray box in the top left corner of the report design, to the left of the horizontal ruler). Then change the Page Header and Page Footer settings to indicate where you want the page header and footer to print, as follows:

✦ **All Pages:** Prints on all pages

✦ **Not with Rpt Hdr:** Does not print on the same page as the report header

✦ **Not with Rpt Ftr:** Does not print on the same page as the report footer

✦ **Not with Rpt Hdr/Ftr:** Does not print on the same page as either the report header or the report footer

## Changing the size of a section

You can change the size of a section easily. Move the mouse pointer to the bottom edge of the section; the pointer turns into a funny-looking double-headed arrow. When you see the new pointer shape, click and drag the border up or down to make the section smaller or larger.

## Controlling the properties of a section

Each section of a report has properties that you can modify. To display the properties for a section, double-click the section selector (*see also* "Selecting Parts of the Report," later in this part). Or you can right-click the gray bar for the section and choose Properties from the shortcut menu.

A dialog box pops up, which lets you view and modify the properties for a section. (Report header, report footer, page header, and page footer sections have fewer properties than other sections.)

```
Section: GroupHeader0                              [X]
Format  Data   Event   Other     All
Name . . . . . . . . . .   GroupHeader0
Force New Page . . . .     None
New Row Or Col . . . .     None
Keep Together . . . . .    Yes
Visible . . . . . . . . .   Yes
Can Grow . . . . . . . .   No
Can Shrink . . . . . . .   No
Repeat Section . . . . .   No
Height . . . . . . . . . .  0.25"
Back Color . . . . . . .   16777215
Special Effect . . . . . .  Flat
Tag . . . . . . . . . . .
On Format . . . . . . .
On Print . . . . . . . .
On Retreat . . . . . .
```

Use the All tab if you want to see all the settings in any properties dialog box. The other tabs show a subset of settings related to the title of the tab.

The following table describes the most useful section properties:

| Property | What It Does |
|---|---|
| Name | Displays the name that Access has given the section |
| Force New Page | Allows you to tell Access to start a new page before this section or after this section |
| New Row or Col | Works like the Force New Page setting when you're printing the report in columns |
| Keep Together | Allows Access to put page breaks where they occur naturally (No) or forces Access to keep the entire section on one page (Yes) |
| Visible | Does what it sounds like; set this property to No if you don't want to see the section |
| Can Grow | Designates whether the section can get larger to accommodate more data in a field in the section (the field control Can Grow property must also be set to Yes) |
| Can Shrink | Enables the section to get smaller if the space is not needed; used in conjunction with the Can Shrink setting for a control |
| Tag | Stores additional identifying information about the section |

# Editing Objects in a Report

To edit any part of a report, you first must display the report in Design view, which you can accomplish by taking one of the following actions:

✦ Select the report in the Reports tab of the Database window and then click the Design button

✦ Click the View: Design button when you preview the report

To edit any object in a report, you first have to select it. Clicking an object is the best way to select it. *See also* "Selecting Parts of a Report," later in this part.

You can change the wording of a label by selecting the label control and then clicking the label again or pressing F2. Access displays a pop-up box with a cursor — use Del and Backspace to delete un-needed characters and type any new characters. Press Enter to put the changes on the report; press Esc to cancel your edits.

You may also want to use the control's properties to edit it. To display the properties for a control, double-click the control, or select it and click the Properties button on the toolbar. You see different properties depending on the type of control you're working with. The following table lists the properties that you're likely to find useful:

| Control Property | What It Does |
| --- | --- |
| Name | Displays the name of the control. |
| Caption | Displays the contents of a label control. |
| Control Source | Displays the name of the field displayed in the control. |
| Format | Displays the format option for the control. |
| Can Grow | Allows the control to grow vertically when the data doesn't fit in the space allotted. When Can Grow is set to No, only the data that fits in the allotted space appears on the report. |
| Can Shrink | Allows the control to shrink when less space is needed to display the data. |

You can delete any object in a report by selecting it and then pressing the Del key.

You may also want to change the font, font size, or alignment of a control. For details, *see also* "Changing Font and Font Size," "Creating a Report Using Design View," and "Aligning Report Objects," in this part. For instructions on moving or changing the size of a control, *see also* "Changing the Size of an Object" and "Moving an Object," both in this part.

# *Formatting Reports with AutoFormat*

With AutoFormat, you can apply the same predefined formats that you saw in the Report Wizard to your report. You have to tell Access which part of the report you want to format — you can choose the whole report, one section, or even just one control.

Here's how to use AutoFormat to format your report:

*1.* Display the report in Design view.

*2.* Select the part of the report that you want to format with AutoFormat.

*See also* "Selecting Parts of a Report," later in this part.

*3.* Click the AutoFormat button.

Access displays the AutoFormat dialog box.

*4.* Choose the format you want from the Report AutoFormats list.

*5.* Click OK to apply the format to the selected part of the report.

Some additional options appear in the AutoFormat dialog box. If you click the Options button, Access displays check boxes that allow you to choose which attributes from the AutoFormat you want to apply: Font, Color, and Border. The default is to apply all three, but you can choose not to apply the fonts, colors, or borders in the AutoFormat to your report by clicking to remove the check mark from the formatting option you don't want Access to apply to your report.

The Customize button displays the Customize AutoFormat dialog box, where you can create and delete AutoFormats. You can create your own format based on the current format of the selection or change the AutoFormat so that it matches the format of the current selection.

# Inserting Page Breaks in a Report

You can add a page break to a report in Design view. Follow these steps:

*1.* Click the Page Break button in the toolbox.

*2.* Move the pointer to the part of the design where you want the page break and click the mouse button.

Access inserts a page break, which looks like a series of dots that are slightly darker than the grid.

Take care where you insert a page break into a report design — you're working with the design, so the break repeats itself. A good place to use a page break is at the end of a section. For example, if you have records grouped by month and you want each month on a separate page, put the page break at the bottom of the Date Footer section in Design view.

# Moving an Object

You can move a control by dragging it. Follow these steps:

*1.* Select the object you want to move.

Anchors appear around the selected object.

***See also*** "Selecting Parts of a Report," in this part.

*2.* Move the mouse pointer to the edge of the box.

The pointer changes into a hand to indicate that you can move the box.

*3.* Click and drag the box where you want the box to appear.

Access gives you some other ways to fine-tune the location of a control in a report. You can do the following things:

✦ Use the grid (the dots) to align a control. If you choose Format⇨ Snap to Grid, Access makes sure that the top left corner of every control lines up with a dot in the grid. If you turn Snap to Grid off (by choosing it again), you can move a control anywhere in the report.

✦ You can align controls by selecting all the objects that you want to align and choosing Format⇨Align. The submenu allows you to align objects by the Left, Right, Top, or Bottom edge. You also can use the submenu to align any selected object To Grid.

✦ Use the horizontal and vertical spacing commands to space a group of selected objects evenly. Select the objects that you want to space evenly; then choose Format⇨Horizontal Spacing⇨Make Equal or Format⇨Vertical Spacing⇨Make Equal.

## Playing with Borders

You can change the appearance of the border surrounding an object not only by changing its color, but also by changing the width and the style of the border.

To change the width of the border (that is, the thickness of the line), follow these steps:

*1.* Select the object.

 *2.* Click the arrow next to the Line/Border Width button.

Access displays a drop-down list of border-width options. The first option is an invisible border.

*3.* Click the border thickness that you want to use.

Access changes the border of the selected object to match the border that you select.

To change the style of the border, use the Special Effects button. Follow these steps:

*1.* Select the object.

 *2.* Click the arrow next to the Special Effects button. Access displays some options.

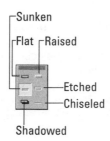

**3.** Click the option that you want to use.

Because the options in the drop-down list don't give you a very good idea of how the option will appear in your report, the best way to see an effect is to try it.

# Previewing Your Report

Reports have two views: Design view and Print Preview. In Design view you tell Access what you want to see in your report, and how you want it organized. Print Preview allows you to see how the report will look on paper.

To display the print preview of a report, click the View button or the Print Preview button on the toolbar.

*See also* "Creating a Report Using Design View," in this part.

*See also* "Previewing Before You Print," in Part VII. Flip to that topic to find out how to navigate your report in Print Preview and how to zoom in and out to see more and less of the report at one time.

# Selecting Parts of a Report

You have to be in Design view to select part of a report. You can select an entire section (such as the Report Header or the Details section) or a single object.

## Selecting controls

Select a *control* (an object in a report) by clicking it. Selected objects have anchors (small black boxes) around them.

You can select more than one control at a time by using the Shift key. Click the first control that you want to select; then hold down the Shift key while you click additional controls. All the selected controls have anchors around them.

You can also select more than one control at a time by clicking the vertical or horizontal ruler. When you click the horizontal ruler at the top of the Design view window, you select all the objects that appear at that point in the design. For instance, if you click at the 1" mark on the ruler, all the objects that appear on the vertical line one inch in from the margin are selected. You can use the vertical ruler on the left of the Design view to select all the objects in one row of the design.

You can also select a control from the Object box in the Formatting toolbar. Click the arrow next to the box to see a list of all objects in the report. Click the control that you want to select. Access displays anchors around that control.

Deselect controls by clicking somewhere in the grid of the design where no control appears. If you want to deselect one of several selected controls, Shift+click the control to deselect it and leave the other controls selected.

### Selecting a section of the report

To select a section of the report, like the Report Header or the Detail section, click the section selector. To select the entire report, click the report selector.

Section selectors

Report selector

# Sending a Report to Another Application

Microsoft has made it very easy for you to send a report (or a datasheet, for that matter) to another Microsoft application. All you need to do is click the OfficeLinks button, which appears on the Print Preview toolbar. The OfficeLinks default application is Word, but you can select Excel from the drop-down list.

When you click the OfficeLinks button, Access saves your report in the format that you've chosen (word processing document or spreadsheet), opens the chosen application, and displays your report. Then you can edit, analyze, or print your report in the other application.

# Sorting Records in a Report

You *can* sort a report by sorting the table or query that generated the fields in the report. But a more foolproof method to sort the report is to use the Sorting and Grouping dialog box.

One method to sort records is to group them. When you tell Access to group by using a certain field, you get sorting thrown in for free. If you want to use a field to sort records without using it to group records, you still get to use the Sorting and Grouping dialog box.

Here's how to use the Sorting and Grouping dialog box to sort the records in a report:

*1.* Display the Sorting and Grouping dialog box by clicking the Sorting and Grouping button on the toolbar.

Access displays the Sorting and Grouping dialog box, with fields used for grouping marked by the grouping icon.

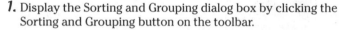

*2.* Click a blank row, and add a field that you want to use for sorting by selecting it from the drop-down list.

*3.* If you don't want to sort in ascending order, press Tab to move to the Sort Order setting and choose Descending from the drop-down list.

*4.* Close the dialog box.

By not giving the field a group header or footer, you use it only for sorting, not for grouping.

# Undoing Formatting

Formatting requires a great deal of experimentation — and sometimes, you'll try something that you wish you hadn't. That's the perfect opportunity to try the Undo button, which undoes the last action that you performed. When you move the mouse pointer to the Undo button, it gives you a hint about what that last thing was. Undo Typing, for example, indicates that when you click the Undo button, Access undoes the typing that you just entered.

You can click the Undo button more than once to undo more than one action.

Instead of clicking the Undo button, you can choose Edit➪Undo or press Ctrl+Z.

# Part VI

# Forms for Displaying and Entering Data

Tables are a great way to store data, but they aren't always great tools when you want to *enter* data — particularly related data that you want to store in separate tables. That's when you need a form.

Unlike tables, forms display only the fields you want to see. You can create a format that shows all the data for one record on the screen at one time — something that is difficult to do when you have a number of fields in a table. You can also add features such as check boxes and drop-down lists that make entering data easier.

## In this part . . .

✔ **Creating AutoForms**

✔ **Formatting a form with AutoFormat**

✔ **Entering data in a form**

✔ **Creating a form with the Form Wizard**

✔ **Refining your form in Design view**

# About Forms

Forms are similar to reports, except that *forms* enable you to work with your data, not just view and print it. You can easily create a form that enables you to work with linked tables — you can see and enter related data in the same place, and you can see all the fields in one record at the same time, instead of having to scroll across a table. You can also create different forms for different people or groups of people who use a database.

Forms can range from relatively simple to complex. Really extravagant forms can include formatting, calculated fields, and controls (such as check boxes, buttons, and pictures) that make entering data easier.

***See also*** Part V. Forms are so similar to reports that many of the skills you use to create a form are the same skills you use to create a report.

# Creating a Form

Making a new form is similar to making any new Access object. The easiest way to create a new form is to follow these steps:

1. Click the Database Window button to display the Database window, and then click the Forms tab.

2. Click the New button.

   Access displays the New Form dialog box, which gives you several choices for creating your form.

   | New Form | ? X |
   | --- | --- |
   | Create a new form without using a wizard. | Design View<br>Form Wizard<br>AutoForm: Columnar<br>AutoForm: Tabular<br>AutoForm: Datasheet<br>Chart Wizard<br>PivotTable Wizard |
   | Choose the table or query where the object's data comes from: | |
   | | OK    Cancel |

3. Pick the method that you want to use to create the form.

4. Select the table or query on which you want to base the form.

5. Click OK.

To help you decide how you want to create a form, the following table describes the choices in the New Form dialog box and explains when to use each of them:

| Type of New Form | When to Use It |
| --- | --- |
| Design View | Use this type when you want to design your own form from scratch, with no help from Access. (Design view is great for putting your own stamp on a form, but getting started with a wizard really helps.) |
| Form Wizard | Use this type when you want help creating a form. The Form Wizard walks you through the creation of a form, enabling you to use fields from multiple tables and queries, to create groups, and to perform calculations for summary fields. The resulting form is bland, but editing an existing form is much easier than creating one from scratch. |
| AutoForm: Columnar | Use this type when you want to create a quick and easy columnar form (the field names go in one column and the data in another) from the table or query that you specify. |
| AutoForm: Tabular | Use this type when you want to create a quick and easy tabular form from the table or query that you specify. A tabular form displays data in rows, like a datasheet, but with more room for each row. |
| AutoForm: Datasheet | Use this type when you want to create a datasheet form from the table or query that you specify. These forms look almost exactly like a datasheet. (Tabular AutoForms are similar, but a little spiffier.) |
| Chart Wizard | Use this type when you want to create a form consisting of a chart. |
| PivotTable Wizard | Use this type when you want to create a form with an Excel PivotTable. |

You don't have to use the New button in the Forms tab of the Database window to create a new form; you can also use the New Object button. In fact, the default setting for the New Object button is an AutoForm. You can also display the button's drop-down list and choose Form. The AutoForm option creates a columnar AutoForm from the data in the table or query that's selected in the Database window.

The quick way to create a form from a table or query is to select the name of the table or query that you want to use in the Database window and then click the New Object button and select Form or AutoForm.

Choosing Insert⇨Form or Insert⇨AutoForm also creates a new form.

## Creating a form using the Form Wizard

The Form Wizard is a great way to create a simple or complex form — but especially a complex form. If you want to use fields from multiple tables in your form, the Form Wizard is the way to go.

*See also* "Working with Wizards," in Part I.

Here's how to create a form using the Form Wizard:

**1.** Display the New Form dialog box and choose Form Wizard.

You don't have to pick a table or query, although you can if you're using fields from only one table or query.

**2.** Click the OK button.

Access displays the first window of the Form Wizard, where you can choose the fields that you want to use in the form.

**3.** Use the Tables/Queries drop-down list to choose the first table or query from which you want to use fields.

**4.** Select the fields in the Available Fields list that you want to appear on the form and move them to the Selected Fields list by double-clicking, or by selecting a field and clicking the right-arrow button.

**5.** Repeat Steps 3 and 4 to select fields from other tables or queries.

**6.** When all the fields that you want to display in the form appear in the Selected Fields box, click Next.

The Form Wizard displays the next window. If you've chosen fields from only one table, this window asks you to choose a format for the form — skip right to Step 9. Otherwise, the window asks how you want to group your data.

---

**Form Wizard**

How do you want to view your data?

- by Catalogs
- **by Order Summary**
- by Items ordered

Catalog, OrderPhone #, CustServicePhone #, Fax #, Address1, Address2, City, State, Zip, E-mail, Web Page, Date

Item Description, Item Number, Number of items, Cost per item, Total Cost for Item, Shipping, Memo

○ Form with subform(s)  ○ Linked forms

[ Cancel ]  [ < Back ]  [ Next > ]  [ Finish ]

**7.** Choose the organization that you want for your form.

Grouping items in a form is similar to grouping fields in a report. In the preceding figure, for example, many items are related to a single order, so grouping the data according to the data in the Order Summary table displays the summary information for the order only once, and then shows all the items ordered (grouped by the catalog from which they were ordered) and the specific information about the order.

If you want to see all the fields on the form at one time, click the Form with subform(s) radio button. If you click Linked forms, Access creates a separate form for the detail records. Users can then view this form by clicking a button in the first form. (If you're not sure which option to choose, go for Form with subforms(s).)

To group fields using another table or query, double-click the table or query by which you want to group records.

**8.** Click Next to see the next window.

Access displays a window that enables you to choose the layout for the form or subform, if you are creating one.

**9.** Choose the layout.

You can click a layout option to see what it looks like. If you're not sure which layout to use, stick with Columnar — it's easy to use and easy to edit. If you're working with grouped fields, this window gives you only two options: Tabular and Datasheet.

**10.** Click <u>N</u>ext to see the next window, which enables you to choose a style for the form.

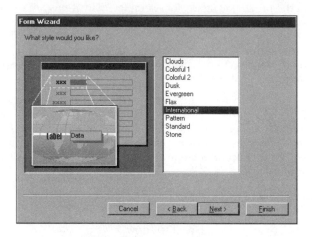

**11.** Choose one of the lovely styles that the Form Wizard offers.

Click a style to see a sample of a form formatted with that style. None of the styles is gorgeous, so pick one and get on with the real work.

**12.** Click <u>N</u>ext to see the final window.

**13.** Give the form a name, and decide whether you want to see the form itself (<u>O</u>pen the form to view or enter information) or the form Design view (<u>M</u>odify the form's design).

If you are creating subforms or linked forms, Access enables you to name those items, too (or you can accept the names that Access gives them).

**14.** Click <u>F</u>inish to create the form.

## Creating a form with an AutoForm

AutoForms are a quick, easy way to create a form that's based on one table or query. AutoForms even know how to handle repeated information which might appear in a query, and they section off the form so that you see the repeated information only once. But AutoForms are easiest to use and understand when you create them using just one table.

Access provides three flavors of AutoForms:

✦ **Columnar:** This type of AutoForm has one record per page.

✦ **Tabular** (not to be confused with *tubular*): Tabular AutoForms are convenient, but I wouldn't go any farther than that. These forms look like generic tables, with field names at the top and the data for each record in a nice, wide row. When you use a Tabular AutoForm, expect to have to do a little resizing of the controls in Design view. Access uses a standard size for the controls — they may not fit your labels and data.

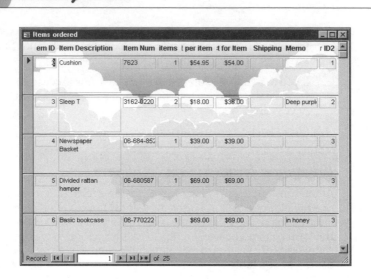

If you use a query that links related data from multiple tables to create a Tabular AutoForm, Access does its best, but the result doesn't look much like a straightforward Tabular AutoForm. If your data comes from more than one table, try the Form Wizard, instead. The Form Wizard enables you to choose how to group repeated data.

✦ **Datasheet:** A Datasheet AutoForm in the following figure looks exactly like a datasheet. This type of AutoForm can be useful for subforms that you want to display in compact list form.

| Item ID | Item Description | Item Number | Numb | Cost per item | Tota |
|---|---|---|---|---|---|
| 3 | Cushion | 7623 | 1 | $54.95 | |
| 3 | Sleep T | 3162-0220 | 2 | $18.00 | |
| 4 | Newspaper Basket | 06-684-852 | 1 | $39.00 | |
| 5 | Divided rattan hamper | 06-680587 | 1 | $69.00 | |
| 6 | Basic bookcase | 06-770222 | 1 | $69.00 | |
| 7 | Bookcase basket | 06-833541 | 1 | $24.00 | |
| 8 | Mortar and Pestle | 81-1066760 | 1 | $29.00 | |
| 9 | Pepper Mill | 81-17574 | 1 | $54.00 | |
| 10 | Brick Doormat | 81-106329 | 1 | $48.00 | |
| 11 | Apple Parer & Slicer | 81-820373 | 1 | $32.00 | |
| 12 | Salad Washer | 81-878041 | 1 | $28.00 | |

To create an AutoForm, follow these steps:

*1.* In the Database window, select the table or query on which you want to base the form.

*2.* To create a Columnar AutoForm, click the New Object: AutoForm button.

Access immediately creates the Columnar AutoForm.

To create another kind of AutoForm, choose _F_orm from the New Object drop-down list.

Access displays the New Form dialog box.

**3.** Choose the type of AutoForm you want to create, and click OK.

Access creates the form.

If you don't like the background that Access chooses for your AutoForm, you can easily change it by using AutoFormat. _See_ "Formatting Your Form with AutoFormat," in this part.

## Creating a form with Subforms

You use subforms when you want to display related data from different tables. The main form in the following figure displays the "one" side of a one-to-many relationship. The subform (the bottom half of the form) displays the records in the "many" side of the relationship.

```
Roster by Class                                    _ □ ×

  Date         9/29/96                 ID:      5

  Class Level  Beginner

  Time         9:00:00 AM

  # attendees  5

  Roster
        First Name            Last Name              ▲
  ▶  Dorothy              Holloway
     Alec                 Aikens
     Zac                  Young                       ▼
  Record: |◄| |◄|       1 |►| |►I| |►*| of 5
Record: |◄| |◄|       3 |►| |►I| |►*| of 37
```

Notice that the form has two navigation bars: one for the main form and one for the subform.

The easiest way to create a form with subforms is to have the Form Wizard do the hard work for you. You can always edit and improve the form later.

If you want to create a main form with a subform, follow these steps:

**1.** Create the main form and display it in Design view.

**2.** Click the Subform/Subreport button in the Toolbox to tell Access that you want to add the subform to the main form.

3. In the form design, click and drag the mouse to create a box in which the subform will appear.

Access launches the Subform/Subreport Wizard to lead you through the process of creating a subform.

# Entering Data in a Form

After you create a form, you want to use it for its intended purpose: viewing and entering data. To use a form that you've created, double-click the form name in the Database window — you're now in Form view. The data that a form displays comes directly from tables in the database, and any changes that you make in that data are reflected in the table. When you add data by using a form, the data is added to the table.

In general, you use the same skills to work with a form as you use to work with datasheets. You can use VCR buttons to move to different records, and you press the Tab or Enter key to move from one field to another. *See also* "Moving Around in a Datasheet," in Part III.

If you prefer to use the keyboard to move around a form, the following table lists the keys to use and where they move the cursor.

| To Move Here in a Form . . . | Press This Key |
| --- | --- |
| Following field | Tab, Enter, or → |
| Preceding field | Shift+Tab or ← |
| First field of current record | Home |
| Last field of current record | End |
| Subform | Ctrl+Tab |
| Main form | Ctrl+Shift+Tab |
| Empty record | Ctrl+plus sign (+) |

You can edit and add records by using a form in Form view. To display a new record, press Ctrl+plus sign (+) or click the New Record button in the toolbar.

# Formatting Your Form with AutoFormat

You can use AutoFormat to give your form one of the format styles that Access provides. The styles you see in the AutoFormat dialog box are the same that you see in the Form Wizard.

To format your form, you first have to select what you want to format: the entire form, part of the form, or even just one control.

Selecting part of a form in Design view is identical to selecting part of a report in Design view. *See also* "Selecting Parts of a Report," in Part V, to brush up on how to select a control or a section of a form or report.

To use AutoFormat to format your form, follow these steps:

*1.* Display the form in Design view.

*2.* Select the part of the form that you want to format with AutoFormat.

*3.* Click the AutoFormat button in the toolbar.

Access displays the AutoFormat dialog box.

*4.* Select the format that you want to use.

You can select a format to see an example of how your form looks formatted.

*5.* Click OK to apply the format to the part of the form that you selected in Step 2.

*See also* "Formatting Reports with AutoFormat," in Part V.

# Inserting Controls

Controls are used in both reports and forms. A *control* is any object that appears in a report or form — it can be a line or text or something that tells Access to display data from a field in a table or query. Controls can also be calculations, pictures, graphs, buttons, and check boxes.

You may want to include types of controls in a form that you wouldn't use in a report — especially list boxes and combo boxes. When you work on your form in Design view, you can display the toolbox, which enables you to make many kinds of controls to put in your form.

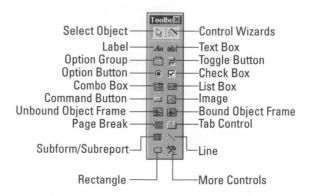

Each button in the toolbox creates a different type of control in the form design. The following table lists the buttons in the toolbox, and what they do to your form.

| Button in the Toolbox | What It Does |
|---|---|
| Label | Creates a box to display text that appears the same for every record. You can attach labels to another control — for example, a text box that contains data from a record. |
| Text Box | Creates a box that displays information from tables and queries in a form. Text boxes display information from a field or the result of a calculation. |
| Option Group | Enables you to create a group of radio buttons in the form so that the user can choose one of several options. |
| Option Button | Creates a single button (like a radio button) that can display a Yes/No value. |
| Check Box | Creates a box that is empty or contains a check mark. Check boxes, like option buttons, enable you to display or input a Yes/No value. |
| Toggle Button | Creates a button that enables you to display or enter data from a Yes/No field. A toggle button displays a default value that changes to the opposite value when the button is clicked. |
| List Box | Creates a box with an arrow at the right end that displays a list of options when clicked. The user must make a choice from the list of options. |
| Combo Box | Creates a box that lets the user select an item from a list or type a new value. |
| Command Button | Creates a button that the user clicks to start an action or set of actions. If you make a command button, you must write a macro or event procedure and attach it to the button's `OnClick` property. |
| Unbound Object | Creates an object that is not bound to a field in the database. An unbound object can display text, a picture, or even a document or spreadsheet created in another application. |
| Bound Object Frame | Creates an object that is bound to a field in the database. If you have a picture of each person in your address book, for example, you may store the filename of the picture in a field in a table and put a bound object frame in the form to display the picture. |
| Page Break | Tells Access to start a new page. |

| Button in the Toolbox | What It Does |
|---|---|
| Subform/Subreport | Inserts another form within the main form. Subforms are useful when you want to show data from a one-to-many relationship .The main form can show the data from the "one" side of the relationship, and the subform can show data from the "many" side of the relationship. |
| Rectangle | Enables you to draw a rectangle in the form. |
| Line | Enables you to draw a line in the form. |
| Image | Displays a picture by using an image file that you specify. |
| Tab Control | Enables you to create tabs (like the ones that some dialog boxes have) to include more than one page of controls in the form. |

*See also* "Creating a Report Using Design View," in Part V.

# Inserting Formulas in Forms

The procedure for putting a calculation in a form is identical to the way you put a calculation in a report. *See also* "Adding Calculations to a Report," in Part V.

# Modifying Tab Order

When entering data in a form, you press Tab to move to the next field. *Tab order* specifies which field the cursor moves to next.

When you create a form, Access designates a tab order. You can change the tab order that Access creates by following these steps:

*1.* Display the form in Design view.

*2.* Choose View⇨Tab Order.

Access displays the Tab Order dialog box.

**3.** Drag the fields so that they appear in the order that is useful for entering data.

**4.** Close the dialog box.

# Selecting Part of a Form

You select part of a form the same way that you select part of a report. First, you must view the form in Design view. *See also* "Selecting Parts of a Report," in Part V.

# Viewing Your Form in Design View

If you want to work on the design of your form, you have to display the form in Design view.

Formatting toolbar

Toolbar                                                          Toolbox

You can display the Design view of a form by doing either of the
following things:

✦ Selecting the form in the Forms tab of the Database window and
   clicking the <u>D</u>esign button

 ✦ Clicking the Design View button when you're working with the
   form in Form view.

The formatting toolbar and the Toolbox also appear in Report Design
view. *See also* "Creating a Report Using Design View," in Part V.

# Part VII

# Printing Your Work for the World to See

Although Access does a marvelous job of giving you results on-screen, you sometimes need to get those results on paper. After all, it's not always convenient to drag your boss out of her office, down the hall, and into your cubicle so that she can see the analysis that she's been bothering you about for so long. You can't get around it — you have to know how to print. And because Access provides so many ways to make an analysis fancy, isn't it appropriate to make the printout look fancy, too?

Printing from Access is fundamentally the same whether you're printing a table, query, form, or report. This part covers all the ins and outs of printing — from previewing your print job to choosing a printer to actually printing your masterpiece — as well as dozens of little extras.

## In this part . . .

- ✔ **Stopping the printer in its tracks**
- ✔ **Setting paper size and orientation**
- ✔ **Previewing your print job**
- ✔ **Printing an object**
- ✔ **Printing only the part you want**

# Canceling a Print Job

If you have a printer directly connected to your computer, you get two chances to cancel a print job. The first chance is when you see a small dialog box telling you that your table (or report or whatever) is printing. The dialog box includes a Cancel button that you can click to cancel the print job.

The printer may continue to print a little longer, but by clicking the Cancel button, you've stopped Access from sending more information to the printer.

If you want to stop a print job after the dialog box with the Cancel button disappears, you have to resort to the fallback method — using the Windows 95 printer window. When any document is printing in Windows 95, a small printer appears in the indicators box in the taskbar. (The *indicators box* usually appears on the right of the taskbar and contains the time.) Double-click that small printer icon to display the Windows 95 Printer window, a window that contains the name of your printer on the title bar and lists current print jobs.

| HP DeskJet 500 | | | | |
|---|---|---|---|---|
| Printer  Document  View  Help | | | | |
| Document Name | Status | Owner | Progress | Started At |
| Classes | Printing | ALISON | 0 of 1 pages | 5:10:16 PM 9/27/96 |
| 1 jobs in queue | | | | |

If the printer you use is on a network, you may not be able to use the Printer window to cancel a print job. You should identify your network guru (or someone who knows how to cancel print jobs) to find out how to cancel a print job on your network.

To cancel a print job from the Printer window, follow these steps:

**1.** Click the print job that you want to cancel.

**2.** Right-click the print job to display the shortcut menu.

**3.** Choose Cancel Printing from the shortcut menu.

The printer stops printing.

# Changing Margins

You can change the margins of your printout by using the Page Setup dialog box.

You can display the Page Setup dialog box in two ways:

✦ Click the Setup button in the Print dialog box.

✦ Choose File⇨Page Setup.

To change margins, view the object you want to print and follow these steps:

*1.* Display the Page Setup dialog box and click the Margins tab.

*2.* Click the setting for the margin that you want to change.

*3.* Edit the value.

You don't have to type the inch marks; Access adds them for you.

*4.* If you want to change another margin, press Tab to move the cursor to another margin setting.

When you move to another option, the sample area of the Page Setup dialog box updates to show you how your new margin looks on paper.

*5.* Choose OK when you finish with the Page Setup dialog box.

# Choosing Paper Size and Orientation

The Page tab of the Page Setup dialog box has settings that tell Access what size paper you're using and whether you want to print in portrait or landscape mode. You can use the Page Setup dialog box to choose options for each object in the database you want to print.

Something weird is going on in Access. You can display the Page Setup dialog box in two ways, but to see the Page tab, you have to choose File⇨Page Setup. If you click the Setup button in the Print dialog box, the Page tab is not displayed.

## Changing paper size

If you're printing on paper other than the standard 8$^1$/$_2$ x 11-inch size, you have to tell Access about it.

To tell Access about the size of the paper you are printing on, view the object you want to print and follow these steps:

*1.* Choose File⇨Page Setup to display the Page Setup dialog box.

*2.* Click the Page tab at the top of the dialog box.

*3.* Click the arrow to the right of Size, and select the size of paper that you're using.

*4.* Click OK to close the dialog box.

## Choosing landscape or portrait

You can ask Access to print your data on the paper in either of two ways:

✦ **Portrait orientation:** This setting puts the short side of the paper at the top and bottom (like a notepad or this book). Why does Access call this *portrait* orientation? Most portraits are framed so that the sides are longer than the top and bottom.

✦ **Landscape orientation:** This setting puts the long side of the paper at the top and bottom, so that more data fits across the page. Most computer monitors have the equivalent of landscape orientation, and so do most landscape paintings in your local museum — the artist can fit in more land and less sky that way.

To change the orientation of the paper, view the object you want to print and follow these steps:

*1.* Choose File⇨Page Setup to display the Page Setup dialog box.

*2.* Click the Page tab at the top of the dialog box.

**Page Setup**

| Margins | Page |

Orientation

[A] ○ Portrait   [A] ○ Landscape

Paper

Size: Letter 8 1/2 x 11 in

Source: Auto sheet feeder

Printer for Catalogs

○ Default Printer

○ Use Specific Printer    Printer...

[ OK ]    [ Cancel ]

**3.** Click Port_r_ait or _L_andscape, depending on how you want Access to print.

**4.** Click OK to close the dialog box.

# Displaying the Print Dialog Box

The Print dialog box provides settings that control how much of the chosen object to print, how many copies to print, the order in which pages of multiple copies are printed, and the printer you print to.

Display the Print dialog box by choosing File⇨Print.

**Print**

Printer

Name: HP DeskJet 500    [ Properties ]

Status: Default printer; User intervention; 0 documents waiting

Type: HP DeskJet 500

Where: \\Lamb\hp-dj5U0

Comment:    ☐ Print to File

Print Range

● All

○ Pages From: ____ To: ____

○ Selected Record(s)

Copies

Number of Copies: 1

☑ Collate

[ Setup... ]    [ OK ]    [ Cancel ]

# Fixing Printer Problems

A printer needs to be both on and online to print. *On* is fairly obvious — your printer has an off/on switch, which you should already be familiar with. *Online,* in this context, means that the printer is ready to accept information from your computer. Most printers have an online light and an online button. Often when your printer won't print, pressing the online button when the online light is off is the easy solution.

Most printer problems fall into a few basic categories:

◆ **Things that the printer needs in order to print aren't there.** Printers need paper and ink or toner to print. If any of these supplies has run out, your printer will be uncooperative.

◆ **The plugs got loose somehow.** Several plugs have to be well connected in order for your printer to work. The cable that plugs the printer into the electrical outlet in your wall is an obvious one, but that same cable often has a plug on the printer end, too. Also check the cable that connects the printer to the computer. Shut down Windows and turn off your computer, and then check the cable at both ends. Gently wiggle the connections to make sure that they're firmly attached.

Be sure to shut down your computer properly and turn it off before messing around with any cables. Plugging in or unplugging your cables while your computer's running could damage your system.

◆ **The printer's already busy.** If the printer is actually printing something else, it won't be able to print what you want. Chances are that your print job is waiting in line — you just have to be patient.

◆ **The printer is jammed or otherwise broken.** Paper sometimes (or often, depending on your printer) gets stuck in printers. To get the printer to work, you have to take the paper out — and you need to get all of it. One little torn piece can make a printer very upset.

If you've checked all the problems in the preceding list and still can't get the printer to print, your printer may be broken. Find an expert to give you a second opinion.

# Picking a Printer

If you have multiple printers set up and attached to your computer (perhaps through a network), you can choose the Name option on the Print dialog box to tell Access which printer to print to. Press Ctrl+P to display the Print dialog box and then click the arrow to the right of the Name option and choose the printer that you want to use.

# *Previewing Before You Print*

Always preview before you print. Previewing your work enables you to make sure that the printout is going to look the way you expect it to — you can save a lot of trees that way!

 To preview your print job, click the Print Preview button.

**TIP** Clicking the Print Preview button when you're working with a report is the same as viewing the report — reports are either in Design or Print Preview view.

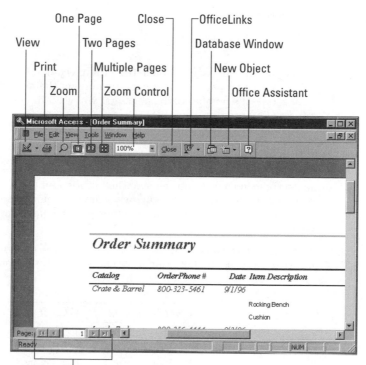

VCR Navigation buttons

 You can click the View button while you're viewing a print preview to see the object in another view — Datasheet view for tables and queries, and Design view for reports and forms.

## *Navigating a preview*

You can get around a print preview in a few ways:

◆ Use the scroll bars, when they appear. (Scroll bars appear only when an entire page doesn't fit on the screen.)

+ Use the ↑, ↓, ←, and → or the PgUp and PgDn keys on the keyboard.

+ Use the VCR navigation buttons at the bottom of the window to view a different page.

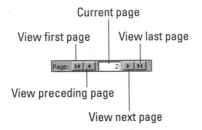

Current page

View first page | View last page

View preceding page

View next page

+ Use the Current page option in the VCR navigation buttons to go to a particular page — just select the number that appears in the box, type the number of the page that you want to view, and press Enter to view the page.

## Zooming in

You can control how big the pages look in print preview. You may want to zoom in so that you can see whether the font looks good and the figures are exactly right, or you may want to zoom out and see a few pages at the same time to see whether you like the general layout.

Four buttons in the toolbar change the amount of the printout that appears on-screen. The following table shows you the buttons and tells you what each button does to the preview.

| Button | What It's Called | What It Does |
|--------|------------------|--------------|
| 🔍 | Zoom | Toggles between 100% and One Page view |
| ▣ | One Page | Displays one entire page in the preview window |
| ▣▣ | Two Pages | Displays two pages in the preview window |
| ▦ | Multiple Pages | Enables you to select from a grid how many pages to display; drag the mouse pointer past the edge of the grid to display a larger grid |
| Fit ▼ | Zoom Control | Enables you to choose your own zoom factor |

To use the Multiple Pages button, follow these steps:

*1.* Click the button.

Access displays a grid of pages.

*2.* Move the mouse pointer so that the number of pages that you want to display are selected.

The bottom of the grid tells you how pages are displayed — for example, 2 x 3 displays two rows of three pages each.

The Zoom button enables you to choose among many zoom levels. The larger the zoom percentage, the larger the print appears on-screen — 100 percent is approximately the size that the print will appear on paper. If you choose Fit from the Zoom drop-down list, Access fits one page in the window. You can change the zoom value by doing either of the following things:

✦ Selecting a value from the drop-down list.

✦ Typing a new zoom value in the box and pressing Enter (you don't have to type %). You can choose zoom values of more than 100 percent by typing them.

# Printing an Object

 Views that you can print have a Print button in the toolbar. Some views (notably Design views) cannot be printed. In those views, the Print button is grayed out, indicating that you can't click it.

 Although you can't print the Design view of a table, query, report, or form, you can print definitions for these objects. Choose Tools⇨ Analyze⇨Documenter to open the Documenter dialog box. *See also* "Using the Documenter," in Part VIII.

You can print an object such as a datasheet or a report in three ways:

✦ To print the object you're viewing immediately, without changing any settings, click the Print button.

✦ If you want to change some settings in the Print dialog box before printing the object that you're viewing, choose File⇨ Print or press Ctrl+P. Change settings as necessary and click OK to print the object.

✦ To print an object without opening it, select it in the Database window and then click the Print button, or right-click the object and then choose Print from the shortcut menu. Access sends the object straight to the printer. To display the Print dialog box first, select the object, and choose File⇨Print. Change settings as necessary and click OK to print the object.

# Printing and Collating Multiple Copies

If you want to print more than one copy, you can use the Print dialog box to tell Access how many copies to print. Just change the setting of the Number of Copies option.

To change the order in which Access prints the pages, use the Collate option.

+ When you select the Collate option, Access prints a single copy of all the pages before moving on to the next copy.

+ When you deselect the Collate option, Access prints multiple copies of the first page before moving on to the second page, and so on.

# Printing Part of an Object

The Print dialog box has a group of options labeled Print Range. These options help you print only what you want.

### Printing specific pages

If you know exactly which pages you want to print, you can use the Print Range option in the Print dialog box to tell Access which pages to print.

To print specific pages, follow these steps:

*1.* Display the Print dialog box by choosing File⇨Print.

*2.* In the Print Range section, choose Pages.

*3.* In the From box, type the number of the first page in the range that you want to print.

*4.* In the To box, type the number of the last page in the range that you want to print.

*5.* Click the OK button to print the pages that you specified.

### Printing specific records

Depending on the object that you're printing, you can print specified records. Here's how to print just the records you want:

*1.* Select the records that you want to print.

*2.* Display the Print dialog box by choosing File⇨Print.

**3.** In the Print Range section, choose Selected <u>R</u>ecords.

If you didn't select any records in Step 1, Access prints the record that the cursor was in when you displayed the Print dialog box.

**4.** Click OK to print the records.

# Part VIII

# *Access 97 Tips and Tricks*

Pick a way to break up a subject, and some useful items always fall through the cracks. Computer-book authors either stick those topics in places where they really don't fit, or they create a separate chapter (or, in this case, a part) on those useful tips and tricks.

## *In this part . . .*

- ✔ **Cutting and pasting**
- ✔ **Exporting information from your database to another application**
- ✔ **Backing up your database**
- ✔ **Checking the spelling of data**
- ✔ **Getting more help with Access**

# Backing Up Your Database

Having a back-up plan for your computer is a necessity, not an option. If you work at home or if you're in charge of backing up your own work at the office, you may want to look at *Windows 95 For Dummies*, 2nd Edition.

In the meantime, at least make back-up copies of your Access databases. Each database is stored in a file on a disk, probably your hard disk. Access files have the extension .mdb, the file type Microsoft Access Database, and are usually stored in the C:\My Documents folder, unless you specify that they be stored somewhere else. The easiest way to create a backup of a database is to simply copy the .mdb file (and the .ldb file, if one exists) to a floppy disk or to another hard disk (perhaps a network drive, if one is available) using Explorer or My Computer. If you can't fit the entire file on one floppy disk, try using a utility like WinZip. WinZip compresses your file and can save it to more than one disk if necessary.

# Cutting, Copying, and Pasting

Cutting and pasting (or copying and pasting) is a great way to move or copy information from one place in Access to another.

You can use the Cut, Copy, and Paste commands in three ways: by clicking buttons in the toolbar, by choosing commands from the Edit menu, or by pressing shortcut keys. The following table lists menu options, buttons, and keystrokes for cutting, copying, and pasting.

| Edit Menu Option | Button | Keystroke |
| --- | --- | --- |
| Cut | ✂ | Ctrl+X |
| Copy | 📋 | Ctrl+C |
| Paste | 📋 | Ctrl+V |

To copy or cut and paste something, follow these steps:

*1.* Select the data or object that you want to cut or copy.

*2.* Choose your favorite method to cut or copy what you selected (Ctrl+X and Ctrl+C are mine).

When you cut something, it disappears from the screen and is stored in the Windows Clipboard. When you copy something, it stays where it is, and Access also places a copy in the Windows Clipboard.

**3.** Move the cursor to the place where you want the item to appear.

**4.** Choose your favorite method to paste the item there (Ctrl+V works well).

# Checking Your Spelling

Spelling seems like such a minor thing. After all, you may think, people know what you *mean*. But misspellings in your reports or forms can make an otherwise careful job look unprofessional.

When Access checks spelling, it compares the data in your database with its own dictionary. (That is, Access checks the words in fields and records — you can't check the spelling of labels in forms and reports, or the spelling of field names.

The fact that Access says a word is misspelled doesn't mean that it actually *is* misspelled — the word may be spelled perfectly but is not in the Access dictionary.

You can check the spelling of data in a datasheet, form, or query. Here's how:

**1.** Click the Database Window button on the toolbar to display the Database window.

**2.** Select a table, form, or query.

**3.** Click the Spelling button in the toolbar.

Access opens the object and displays the Spelling dialog box with the first word that it thinks is misspelled.

| Spelling | ? X |
|---|---|
| Not In Dictionary: Dodgeville | |
| Change To: Dodgeville | |
| Suggestions: (No Suggestions) | Ignore 'City' Field |
| | Ignore    Ignore All |
| | Change    Change All |
| | Add    Suggest |
| Add Words To: Custom.Dic | |
| AutoCorrect    Options...    Undo Last    Cancel | |

**4.** To correct the word displayed in the Not In Dictionary box, choose a correctly spelled word from the Suggestions list or type a correctly spelled word in the Change To box and then click Change.

Access corrects the misspelled word and looks for the next misspelled word.

You can use buttons in the Spelling dialog box to do much more than just correct spelling. The following table describes what each button does.

| Button | What It Does |
| --- | --- |
| Ignore "Fieldname" Field | Tells Access not to check the spelling of the specified field |
| Ignore | Skips the current word and finds the next misspelled word |
| Ignore All | Ignores the word listed in the Not In Dictionary box each time it is found during the current spelling check |
| Change | Changes the word in the Not In Dictionary box to the word listed in the Change To box |
| Change All | Changes the word in the Not In Dictionary box to the word listed in the Change To box every time it is found during the current spelling check |
| Add | Adds the word to the dictionary |
| Suggest | Suggests more words |
| AutoCorrect | Adds the misspelled word and the correct spelling to the AutoCorrect list |
| Options | Displays the Spell Options dialog box where you can tell Access whether to suggest words, whether to ignore certain words, and which dictionary to use (specify a foreign language using the Dictionary option) |
| Undo Last | Undoes the last change made in the Spelling dialog box |
| Cancel | Closes the Spelling dialog box |

# Importing and Exporting Data

You may want to get data stored in another application and use it in your Access database. Conversely, you may want to use data from Access in another application. For example, all your data may be stored in an Excel or Lotus 1-2-3 worksheet. Rather than retyping all that data, you can *import* the data into Access. Or you may want to use the data you've stored in Access in a statistical analysis package that uses .xls files. You can *export* the data to an .xls file.

## Using an Access object in another database or program

If you need to use an object from one database in another database, you can easily export the object to another file. Using the same technique, you can export an object from an Access database to a file that isn't an Access file — a FoxPro or Excel file, for example.

To export an object, follow these steps:

*1.* Open the database that contains the object.

*2.* Select the object in the Database window.

*3.* Choose File⇨Save As/Export, or right-click the object and then choose Save As/Export from the shortcut menu. Access displays the Save As dialog box.

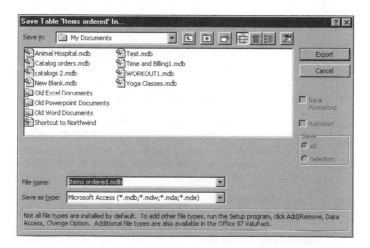

*4.* Choose To an External File or Database.

*5.* Click OK. Access displays a version of the Save dialog box in which you can navigate folders to find the database to which you want to export the object.

**6.** Select the file type that you want to create or export to using the Save as type drop-down list.

If you're saving to an Access database, you can skip this step — Access databases are the default file type.

**7.** Select the file to which you want to save the object by typing the name in the File name box. You can save to an Access file that already exists, or you can create a completely new file by typing a new name in the File name box. If you're creating a non-Access file, type a name for your brand-new file.

**8.** Click the Export button.

If you're exporting to a file type other than an Access database, the object is exported. If you're exporting to another Access file, you see the Export dialog box, where you can rename the object (if you want to) and tell Access whether you want to export all the data or just the object definition (field names, format, and any expressions).

**9.** Make any changes that you need to make in the Export dialog box.

**10.** Click OK.

Access quietly completes the export process.

To see whether the operation worked, open the file to which you exported the object.

## Using data from an outside source

You can use data from an existing file in two ways: Import it or link to it. *Importing* means bringing the data into your database — as if you'd typed all the data into Access yourself, but without the work. *Linking* means that Access goes back to that other file to find the data. You can change the data in the other file and see the changes reflected in your database.

The easiest way to link or import data is to use the Import Data Wizard or the Link Table Wizard. These wizards enable you to see what you're working with and give you more options than importing or linking with a simple menu command. The wizards know how to deal with multiple worksheets in an Excel file, for example. You can even choose to import only selected parts of the data.

Open the database that you want to contain the imported or linked data, and follow these steps to import or link data:

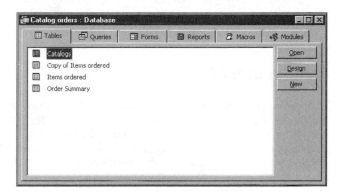

**1.** Click <u>N</u>ew in the Tables tab of the Database window and choose Import Table or Link Table from the New Table dialog box.

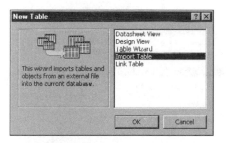

Access displays the Import or Link dialog box, where you specify the name of the file that contains the data you're importing or linking to.

**2.** Use the Files of type drop-down menu to choose the file type that you're importing from.

For example, if you're importing data from an Excel file, choose Microsoft Excel (*.xls). Access then displays the Excel files in the current folder.

**3.** Navigate the folder structure on the disk (if necessary) to find the file that contains the data you want to use in the database you have open. Click the file name so that it appears in the File <u>n</u>ame box on the Import or Link dialog box.

**4.** Click either the Import button or the Link button — the Import button if you're importing data, the Link button if you're linking data. (The name of the button depends on whether you chose Import Data or Link Data in Step 1).

**5.** The appropriate wizard takes over and guides you through the process of choosing the data you want to import or link to. The windows you see depend on the type of file that contains the data you're importing or linking to.

# Using the Documenter

Documentation is an important part of any database. Few people stay at the same job forever, and even when they do, they may not remember everything. So if you don't have the time or the inclination to make a note of how your database works, the Documenter is a great way to get a good start on documenting your database.

To use the Documenter, follow these steps:

**1.** Choose Tools⇨Analyze⇨Documenter.

Access displays the Documenter dialog box, which lists the objects in your database.

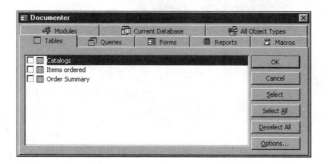

**2.** Choose the objects that you want Access to document by clicking the appropriate check boxes.

If you click the All Object Types tab of the dialog box, you can choose among all the objects in the database. You can also use the Select All button to select all the objects in the database.

**3.** Click OK to start the Documenter. (If you've selected many objects, the Documenter may take a while.)

The Documenter creates a report that will *not* be stored in the database.

The Documenter creates a report like the one pictured here:

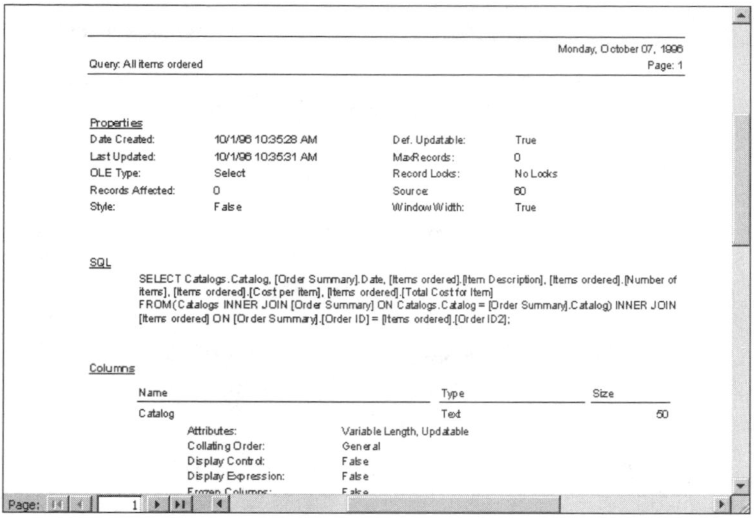

To create a printout of the report, click the Print button. You can also click the OfficeLinks: Word button to create a Word document form of the documentation.

# Using Other Access Resources

Although this Quick Reference is useful, if you do significant work with Access, you may need other references. Particularly if you're building databases, you may find that you need more hints on how to proceed than this book can give you. Some other resources may be useful to you.

IDG Books Worldwide, Inc., publishes other books about Access, including the following:

✦ *Dummies 101: Access 97 For Windows:* If you want a step-by-step tutorial, this book is a good investment. It walks you through the basics of creating and using a simple database.

✦ *Access 97 For Windows For Dummies:* This book is a good all-around reference for the beginning and intermediate Access user.

✦ *Access 97 Bible:* This book covers all the bases — it starts with basic information but also includes more advanced skills. *Access 97 Bible* is a great reference and tutorial (it even comes with a CD-ROM) for the intermediate to advanced user.

If you're an Internet user, you can find some Access resources on the World Wide Web. The following are some good places to start:

✦ Microsoft has some useful examples of Access databases at `http://www.microsoft.com`.

✦ Many online services have discussion groups about Microsoft software. Check with your Internet service provider to see whether they have newsgroups or forums dedicated to Microsoft Access.

✦ Do a search for the word *Microsoft Access,* using your favorite search engine. Many sites provide hints on using Access 97.

# Techie Talk

**cell:** The intersection of a row and a column in a datasheet. A cell holds the information in one field for one record.

**click:** To move the mouse pointer to something and press the left mouse button.

**control:** Any object that appears in a report or form. A control can be a line, text, or something that tells Access to display data from a field in a table or query.

**cursor:** The marker that tells you where you are on-screen. The cursor is usually a thin vertical black bar, although it can be other shapes.

**data:** Information such as numbers, addresses, dates, and text.

**database:** An organized collection of data. In Access, a database is a file on your hard disk (or wherever you store it) consisting of tables that contain your data and any other objects you have defined (queries, reports, or forms).

**default:** The built-in setting. In a dialog box, the default setting is the one that Access uses unless you tell it to do something different.

**dialog box:** A box of options that Access uses to collect information from you.

**double-click:** To move the mouse pointer to something and press the left mouse button twice, in quick succession. You must be careful not to move the mouse pointer between clicks.

**drag and drop:** A method of moving items from one place on-screen to another. To drag and drop an item, move the mouse pointer to the item, hold down the left mouse button, move the item to the new position, and release the mouse button.

**drop-down menu/list:** A list of options that you can choose.

**dynaset:** The data that results from a query. A dynaset is usually displayed in Datasheet view.

**field:** A category of data in your database. Each field in your database stores one kind of data. You may have a field called Last Name, for example, which stores the last names of all the people in the database. In a table, fields are the columns.

**font:** A style of type. A font is made up of letters and other characters.

**footer:** Text or other information that appears at the bottom of each printed page.

**header:** Text or other information that appears at the top of each printed page.

**hot key:** The underlined letter on a button or in a menu command. You can press the Alt key in combination with the hot key to perform the command without using the mouse.

**mouse pointer:** The thing (usually an arrow) on-screen that moves when you move the mouse.

**object:** Part of an Access database. The types of objects that make up an Access database are tables, reports, queries, and forms.

**primary key:** The field that uniquely identifies each record in a table.

**query:** The tool you use to get information from your database. You can use a query to select particular records from the database and to create summary calculations, as well as to delete or change records, or make a new table.

**radio button:** A circle with a dot in it, usually in a dialog box, that shows whether an option is chosen. Radio buttons come in groups, and you can only choose one button in the group at a time. To turn off one choice, click another radio button in the same group.

**record:** A group of fields of related information. One record may consist of a person's name, address, and other information that you want to store. In a table, records are the rows.

**right-click:** To move the mouse pointer to something and press the right mouse button.

**scroll:** To view more information on-screen by using the scroll bars, arrow keys, PgUp and PgDn keys, or other navigation keys.

**select:** To choose. The easiest way to select something is to click it. Selected items are usually highlighted. Occasionally (depending on what is being selected), you may have to click at the beginning of the item to be highlighted and drag the mouse pointer to the end.

**shortcut menu:** The menu that appears when you right-click. Shortcut menus give you a way to quickly find commands that are relevant to the task you're working on.

**taskbar:** The Windows 95 feature that displays a button for each program running. The taskbar usually appears on the bottom edge of the screen, although you can move it to any edge. To use the taskbar, click the button for the program you want to display.

**toggle:** A key or option that switches between two or more settings. To cycle through the possibilities of a toggle option, click the option or press the key. For example, the Insert key is a toggle option — press the key once to change to overstrike mode; press it again to return to insert mode.

**toolbar:** The row of buttons below the menu.

**toolbox:** The box of buttons used for building forms and reports. The toolbox contains a button for each type of object commonly used in a form or report.

**VCR buttons:** Buttons that look like the buttons on a VCR, which help you navigate around an object.

**wizards:** Access tools that lead you step by step through a task by asking questions. The Query Wizard, for example, asks you questions and then builds a query based on your answers.

# Index